Forces

elevate science
MODULES

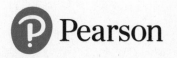 Pearson

Boston, Massachusetts   Chandler, Arizona
Glenview, Illinois   New York, New York

AUTHORS

You're an author!

As you write in this science book, your answers and personal discoveries will be recorded for you to keep, making this book unique to you. That is why you are one of the primary authors of this book.

✏️ **In the space below, print your name, school, town, and state. Then write a short autobiography that includes your interests and accomplishments.**

YOUR NAME ....

SCHOOL ....

TOWN, STATE ....

AUTOBIOGRAPHY ....

....

....

....

....

....

Your Photo

The cover photo shows an orange splashing in water.

Front cover: Orange, Khm Kvch Kan T Silp/EyeEm/Getty Images; Back cover: Science Doodle, LHF Graphics/Shutterstock.

 Pearson

ISBN-13: 978-1-418-29154-9
ISBN-10: 1-418-29154-4
2   18

Program Authors

ZIPPORAH MILLER, Ed.D.
Coordinator for K-12 Science Programs, Anne Arundel County Public Schools
Dr. Zipporah Miller currently serves as the Senior Manager for Organizational Learning with the Anne Arundel County Public School System. Prior to that she served as the K-12 Coordinator for science in Anne Arundel County. She conducts national training to science stakeholders on the Next Generation Science Standards. Dr. Miller also served as the Associate Executive Director for Professional Development Programs and conferences at the National Science Teachers Association (NSTA) and served as a reviewer during the development of Next Generation Science Standards. Dr. Miller holds a doctoral degree from the University of Maryland College Park, a master's degree in school administration and supervision from Bowie State University and a bachelor's degree from Chadron State College.

MICHAEL J. PADILLA, Ph.D.
Professor Emeritus, Eugene P. Moore School of Education, Clemson University, Clemson, South Carolina
Michael J. Padilla taught science in middle and secondary schools, has more than 30 years of experience educating middle-school science teachers, and served as one of the writers of the 1996 U.S. National Science Education Standards. In recent years Mike has focused on teaching science to English Language Learners. His extensive experience as Principal Investigator on numerous National Science Foundation and U.S. Department of Education grants resulted in more than $35 million in funding to improve science education. He served as president of the National Science Teachers Association, the world's largest science teaching organization, in 2005–6.

MICHAEL E. WYSESSION, Ph.D
Professor of Earth and Planetary Sciences, Washington University, St. Louis, Missouri
Author of more than 100 science and science education publications, Dr. Wysession was awarded the prestigious National Science Foundation Presidential Faculty Fellowship and Packard Foundation Fellowship for his research in geophysics, primarily focused on using seismic tomography to determine the forces driving plate tectonics. Dr. Wysession is also a leader in geoscience literacy and education; he is the chair of the Earth Science Literacy Initiative, the author of several popular video lectures on geology in the *Great Courses* series, and a lead writer of the *Next Generation Science Standards**.

REVIEWERS

Program Consultants

Carol Baker
Science Curriculum

Dr. Carol K. Baker is superintendent for Lyons Elementary K-8 School District in Lyons, Illinois. Prior to this, she was Director of Curriculum for Science and Music in Oak Lawn, Illinois. Before this she taught Physics and Earth Science for 18 years. In the recent past, Dr. Baker also wrote assessment questions for ACT (EXPLORE and PLAN), was elected president of the Illinois Science Teachers Association from 2011–2013, and served as a member of the Museum of Science and Industry (Chicago) advisory board. She is a writer of the Next Generation Science Standards. Dr. Baker received her B.S. in Physics and a science teaching certification. She completed her master's of Educational Administration (K-12) and earned her doctorate in Educational Leadership.

Jim Cummins
ELL

Dr. Cummins's research focuses on literacy development in multilingual schools and the role technology plays in learning across the curriculum. *Elevate Science* incorporates research-based principles for integrating language with the teaching of academic content based on Dr. Cummins's work.

Elfrieda Hiebert
Literacy

Dr. Hiebert, a former primary-school teacher, is President and CEO of TextProject, a non-profit aimed at providing open-access resources for instruction of beginning and struggling readers, She is also a research associate at the University of California Santa Cruz. Her research addresses how fluency, vocabulary, and knowledge can be fostered through appropriate texts, and her contributions have been recognized through awards such as the Oscar Causey Award for Outstanding Contributions to Reading Research (Literacy Research Association, 2015), Research to Practice award (American Educational Research Association, 2013), and the William S. Gray Citation of Merit Award for Outstanding Contributions to Reading Research (International Reading Association, 2008).

Content Reviewers

Alex Blom, Ph.D.
Associate Professor
Department Of Physical Sciences
Alverno College
Milwaukee, Wisconsin

Joy Branlund, Ph.D.
Department of Physical Science
Southwestern Illinois College
Granite City, Illinois

Judy Calhoun
Associate Professor
Physical Sciences
Alverno College
Milwaukee, Wisconsin

Stefan Debbert
Associate Professor of Chemistry
Lawrence University
Appleton, Wisconsin

Diane Doser
Professor
Department of Geological Sciences
University of Texas at El Paso
El Paso, Texas

Rick Duhrkopf, Ph.D.
Department of Biology
Baylor University
Waco, Texas

Jennifer Liang
University of Minnesota Duluth
Duluth, Minnesota

Heather Mernitz, Ph.D.
Associate Professor of Physical Sciences
Alverno College
Milwaukee, Wisconsin

Joseph McCullough, Ph.D.
Cabrillo College
Aptos, California

Katie M. Nemeth, Ph.D.
Assistant Professor
College of Science and Engineering
University of Minnesota Duluth
Duluth, Minnesota

Maik Pertermann
Department of Geology
Western Wyoming Community College
Rock Springs, Wyoming

Scott Rochette
Department of the Earth Sciences
The College at Brockport
State University of New York
Brockport, New York

David Schuster
Washington University in St Louis
St. Louis, Missouri

Shannon Stevenson
Department of Biology
University of Minnesota Duluth
Duluth, Minnesota

Paul Stoddard, Ph.D.
Department of Geology and Environmental Geosciences
Northern Illinois University
DeKalb, Illinois

Nancy Taylor
American Public University
Charles Town, West Virginia

Teacher Reviewers

Jennifer Bennett, M.A.
Memorial Middle School
Tampa, Florida

Sonia Blackstone
Lake County Schools
Howey In the Hills, Florida

Teresa Bode
Roosevelt Elementary
Tampa, Florida

Tyler C. Britt, Ed.S.
Curriculum & Instructional
 Practice Coordinator
Raytown Quality Schools
Raytown, Missouri

A. Colleen Campos
Grandview High School
Aurora, Colorado

Ronald Davis
Riverview Elementary
Riverview, Florida

Coleen Doulk
Challenger School
Spring Hill, Florida

Mary D. Dube
Burnett Middle School
Seffner, Florida

Sandra Galpin
Adams Middle School
Tampa, Florida

Margaret Henry
Lebanon Junior High School
Lebanon, Ohio

Christina Hill
Beth Shields Middle School
Ruskin, Florida

Judy Johnis
Gorden Burnett Middle School
Seffner, Florida

Karen Y. Johnson
Beth Shields Middle School
Ruskin, Florida

Jane Kemp
Lockhart Elementary School
Tampa, Florida

Denise Kuhling
Adams Middle School
Tampa, Florida

Esther Leonard, M.Ed. and L.M.T.
Gifted and talented Implementation Specialist
San Antonio Independent School District
San Antonio, Texas

Kelly Maharaj
Challenger K–8 School of Science
 and Mathematics
Spring Hill, Florida

Kevin J. Maser, Ed.D.
H. Frank Carey Jr/Sr High School
Franklin Square, New York

Angie L. Matamoros, Ph.D.
ALM Science Consultant
Weston, Florida

Corey Mayle
Brogden Middle School
Durham, North Carolina

Keith McCarthy
George Washington Middle School
Wayne, New Jersey

Yolanda O. Peña
John F. Kennedy Junior High School
West Valley City, Utah

Kathleen M. Poe
Jacksonville Beach Elementary School
Jacksonville Beach, Florida

Wendy Rauld
Monroe Middle School
Tampa, Florida

Anne Rice
Woodland Middle School
Gurnee, Illinois

Bryna Selig
Gaithersburg Middle School
Gaithersburg, Maryland

Pat (Patricia) Shane, Ph.D.
STEM & ELA Education Consultant
Chapel Hill, North Carolina

Diana Shelton
Burnett Middle School
Seffner, Florida

Nakia Sturrup
Jennings Middle School
Seffner, Florida

Melissa Triebwasser
Walden Lake Elementary
Plant City, Florida

Michele Bubley Wiehagen
Science Coach
Miles Elementary School
Tampa, Florida

Pauline Wilcox
Instructional Science Coach
Fox Chapel Middle School
Spring Hill, Florida

Safety Reviewers

Douglas Mandt, M.S.
Science Education Consultant
Edgewood, Washington

Juliana Textley, Ph.D.
Author, NSTA books on school science safety
Adjunct Professor
Lesley University
Cambridge, Massachusetts

TOPIC 1

Forces and Motion x

MS-PS2-1, MS-PS2-2, MS-PS2-4, MS-PS3-2

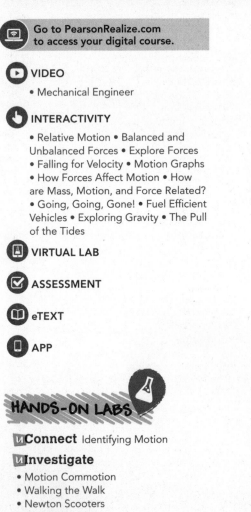

Go to PearsonRealize.com to access your digital course.

VIDEO
- Mechanical Engineer

INTERACTIVITY
- Relative Motion • Balanced and Unbalanced Forces • Explore Forces • Falling for Velocity • Motion Graphs • How Forces Affect Motion • How are Mass, Motion, and Force Related? • Going, Going, Gone! • Fuel Efficient Vehicles • Exploring Gravity • The Pull of the Tides

VIRTUAL LAB

ASSESSMENT

eTEXT

APP

HANDS-ON LABS

uConnect Identifying Motion

uInvestigate
- Motion Commotion
- Walking the Walk
- Newton Scooters
- Observing Friction
- Sticky Sneakers

uDemonstrate
Stopping on a Dime

MS-PS2-3, MS-PS2-5, MS-PS3-2

Go to PearsonRealize.com to access your digital course.

▶ **VIDEO**
- Electrical Engineer

👆 **INTERACTIVITY**
- Theremin
- Electric Currents
- Charged Interactions
- Interactions of Magnetic Fields
- Model Magnetic Forces
- Electricity and Magnetism
- Electromagnetism
- Electromagnetic Evidence
- Electric Motors
- Generators
- Electricity, Magnets, and Motion

📱 **VIRTUAL LAB**

☑ **ASSESSMENT**

📖 **eTEXT**

📱 **APP**

HANDS-ON LABS

uConnect Magnetic Poles

uInvestigate
- Detecting Charges
- Detecting Fake Coins
- Electric Currents and Magnetism
- Electric, Magnetic Motion

uDemonstrate
Planetary Detective

Elevate your thinking!

Elevate Science takes science to a whole new level and lets you take ownership of your learning. Explore science in the world around you. Investigate how things work. Think critically and solve problems! *Elevate Science* helps you think like a scientist, so you're ready for a world of discoveries.

Explore Your World

Explore real-life scenarios with engaging Quests that dig into science topics around the world. You can:

- Solve real-world problems
- Apply skills and knowledge
- Communicate solutions

Make Connections

Elevate Science connects science to other subjects and shows you how to better understand the world through:

- Mathematics
- Reading and Writing
- Literacy

Quest KICKOFF

What do you think is causing Pleasant Pond to turn green?

In 2016, algal blooms turned bodies of water green and slimy in Florida, Utah, California, and 17 other states. These blooms put people and ecosystems in danger. Scientists, such as limnologists, are working to predict and prevent future algal blooms. In this problem-based Quest activity, you will investigate an algal bloom at a lake and determine its cause. In labs and digital activities, you will apply what you learn in each lesson to help you gather evidence to solve the mystery. With enough evidence, you will be able to identify what you believe is the cause of the algal bloom and present a solution in the Findings activity.

Math Toolbox

Graphing Population Changes

Ohio's Deer Population

Changes in a population over time, such as white-tailed deer in Ohio, can be displayed in a graph.

Deer Population Trends, 2000–2010

Year	Population (estimated)	Year	Population (estimated)
2000	525,000	2006	770,000
2001	560,000	2007	725,000
2002	620,000	2008	745,000
2003	670,000	2009	750,000
2004	715,000	2010	710,000
2005	720,000		

Relationships Use the data

800,000

READING CHECK **Determine Central ideas**
What adaptations might the giraffe have that help it survive in its environment?

Academic Vocabulary

Relate the term *decomposer* to the verb *compose*. What does it mean to compose something?

Build Skills for the Future

- Master the Engineering Design Process
- Apply critical thinking and analytical skills
- Learn about STEM careers

Focus on Inquiry

Case studies put you in the shoes of a scientist to solve real-world mysteries using real data. You will be able to:

- Analyze Data
- Test a hypothesis
- Solve the Case

Case Study

MS-LS2-1

THE CASE OF THE DISAPPEARING

Cerulean Warbler

The cerulean warbler is a small, migratory songbird named for its blue color. Cerulean warblers breed in eastern North America during the spring and summer. The warblers spend the winter months in the Andes Mountains of Colombia, Venezuela, Ecuador, and Peru in northern part of South America.

Enter the Lab

Hands-on experiments and virtual labs help you test ideas and show what you know in performance-based assessments. Scaffolded labs include:

- STEM Labs
- Design Your Own
- Open-ended Labs

Model it!

Predator and Prey Adaptations

Figure 4 In a rainforest ecosystem, a gecko finds out that the flexible snake can hold onto tree bark with its muscles and scales as it hunts.

Develop Models Consider a grassland ecosystem of tall, tan savanna grasses. Draw either a predator or a prey organism that might live there. Label the adaptations that will allow your organism to be successful.

HANDS-ON LAB

Investigate Observe how once-living matter is broken down into smaller components in the process of decomposition.

Alike and Different: Living Things

Click the pictures.
Compare how living things and their parents are alike and different.
Write your answer below.

Type your answer here.

Forces and Motion

NGSS PERFORMANCE EXPECTATIONS

MS-PS2-1 Apply Newton's Third Law to design a solution to a problem involving the motion of two colliding objects.

MS-PS2-2 Plan an investigation to provide evidence that the change in an object's motion depends on the sum of the forces on the object and the mass of the object.

MS-PS2-4 Construct and present arguments using evidence to support the claim that gravitational interactions are attractive and depend on the masses of interacting objects.

MS-PS3-2 Develop a model to describe that when the arrangement of objects interacting at a distance changes, different amounts of potential energy are stored in the system.

What forces act on these skydivers?

HANDS-ON LAB

uConnect Determine a reference point for two different observers.

GO ONLINE
to access your
digital course

▶ VIDEO

👆 INTERACTIVITY

📱 VIRTUAL LAB

☑ ASSESSMENT

📖 eTEXT

⚗ HANDS-ON LABS

The Essential Question

How is the motion of an object affected by forces that act on it?

Just for thrills, skydivers leap from a helicopter and fall to the ground. They fall faster and faster until they reach a top speed of 195 km/h (122 mi/h)! Think about the forces that act on the skydivers. Why do they reach a top speed instead of continuing to accelerate?

....

....

....

....

....

Quest KICKOFF

How can you take the crash out of a collision?

Phenomenon When engineers design amusement park rides, they have to consider all of the forces that will be acting on riders and make sure the rides are safe. Engineers test their designs with dummies to ensure that riders will not fall out of their seats and collisions will not be harmful to them. In this problem-based Quest activity, you will apply your knowledge of Newton's laws of motion to design a bumper car ride that is safe—for both the rider and the bumper car. You will explore forces and Newton's third law of motion as you design, build, test, and refine a model bumper car.

 INTERACTIVITY

Build a Better Bumper Car

MS-PS2-1 Apply Newton's Third Law to design a solution to a problem involving the motion of two colliding objects.

NBC LEARN ▶ VIDEO

After watching the Quest Kickoff video, which examines forces and the laws of motion, think about amusement park rides. Complete the 3-2-1 activity.

3 things riders want to experience

....

....

....

2 ways that rides keep riders safe

....

....

1 way in which riders sometimes get injured

....

....

Quest CHECK-IN

IN LESSON 1

STEM What criteria and constraints must engineers consider when designing a safe ride? Think about the goals of the project and how you will ensure a positive outcome.

 **INTERACTIVITY**

Define Criteria and Constraints

Quest CHECK-IN

IN LESSON 2

How do mass and speed affect collisions? Observe and collect data on how mass and speed affect collisions.

HANDS-ON LAB

Mass, Speed, and Colliding Cars

Quest CHECK-IN

IN LESSON 3

STEM How do varying masses and rates of speed affect bumper cars and their riders? Develop and evaluate a design for a safe and fun bumper car.

INTERACTIVITY

Apply Newton's Laws of Motion

Every time a bumper car moves forward and hits another car, there is an equal push in the opposite direction. That is part of what makes riding bumper cars fun.

Quest CHECK-IN

IN LESSON 4

STEM How do the action-reaction forces affect bumper cars and their riders? Build, test, evaluate, and improve your bumper car model.

HANDS-ON LAB

Bumping Cars, Bumper Solutions

Quest FINDINGS

Complete the Quest!

Present your final design and explain how you applied Newton's third law of motion as you developed your design.

INTERACTIVITY

Reflect on Your Bumper Car Solution

Describing Motion and Force

Guiding Questions

• When is an object in motion?
• How do different types of forces affect motion?

Connections

Literacy Draw Evidence

Math Write an Inequality

MS-PS2-2

HANDS-ON LAB

uInvestigate Explore how to tell whether an object you are observing is in motion.

Vocabulary

motion
reference point
force
newton
friction
gravity
net force

Academic Vocabulary

relative

Connect It !

🖋 **What part of the image indicates that there is motion? Label it with the word "motion."**

Constructing Explanations Why did you label that part of the image?

....

....

....

Apply Scientific Reasoning This image shows a car traveling down a road. Why do you think the dog in the car does not appear to be moving?

....

....

....

An Object in Motion

How do you decide whether something is moving? For example, if you were the photographer riding in the car in **Figure 1**, would you say the dog is moving? Parts of it would seem to be. Its eyes blink, and its ears flap in the wind. But to you, the dog would appear to be staying in one position. You know, however, that the dog is in a car that is speeding down the road, so it must be moving. What determines whether the dog is moving or not?

Reference Points An object is in **motion** if its position changes when compared to another object. To decide whether the dog is moving, you might use yourself as a reference point. A **reference point** is a place or object used for comparison to determine whether something is in motion. Objects that are fixed to Earth—such as a tree, a stop sign, or a building—make good reference points. Suppose a tree along the road in **Figure 1** is used as a reference point. The car moves past the tree, as does the dog inside the car. In relation to the tree, the dog changes position, and therefore is in motion. However, if you are the photographer in **Figure 1**, and you are the reference point, your position relative to the dog does not change. You could say that, compared to you, the dog is not in motion.

☑ READING CHECK **Determine Conclusions** Suppose that you are in the car with the dog. What might be your reference point, other than yourself, if you determine that the dog is not moving?

....

....

👆 INTERACTIVITY

Discover how to use reference points.

Movin' Along
Figure 1 The dog is moving in relation to the landscape, but it is not moving in relation to the car.

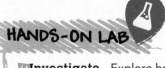

☑**Investigate** Explore how to tell whether an object you are observing is in motion.

Academic Vocabulary

In this lesson, *relative* means "not fixed, not absolute." What does *relative* mean when you use it as a noun?

....

....

....

....

Relative Motion Because motion is determined by a reference point that can change, motion is **relative**. Suppose you are relaxing on a beach. If you use your beach towel as your reference point, you are not moving. You and the beach towel are not changing positions relative to each other. Suppose you use the sun as a reference point instead of your beach towel. If you compare your position to the sun, you are moving quite rapidly, because you are on Earth and Earth revolves around the sun. Relative to the sun, you are moving, but relative to Earth, you are sitting still, so you don't feel as if you are in motion. See **Figure 2** for another example of relative motion.

☑**READING CHECK** **Draw Evidence** What sources of information might you use to determine the relative motion of Earth compared to other planets in the solar system?

....

....

Relative Motion

Figure 2 🖊 Circle the person on the right side of the front car. In the table, list three reference points that could be used to show that the person is in motion. List three reference points that could be used to show that the person is stationary.

In motion relative to...	Stationary relative to...

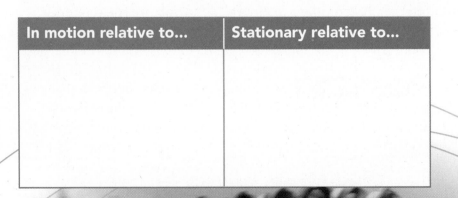

How Forces Affect Motion

While objects move relative to one another, they can also speed up, slow down, and change direction. The motion of an object can change when one or more forces act on the object. A **force** is a push or a pull. When one object pushes or pulls another object, the first object exerts a force on the second object. You exert a force on a book when you push it into your book bag. You exert a force on the sleeve of your jacket when you pull it off your arm.

Describing Force A force is described by its strength and by the direction in which it acts. The force needed to lift a dinner plate requires less strength than the force needed to push a refrigerator. Pushing a faucet handle to the left is a different force from pushing it to the right. In an image, the direction and strength of a force acting on an object can be represented by an arrow. The arrow points in the direction of the force, as shown in **Figure 3**. The length of the arrow indicates the strength of the force—the longer the arrow, the greater the force. In the International System of Units (SI), the unit for the strength of a force is called a **newton** (N), after the scientist Sir Isaac Newton.

A bird sits on top of an elephant.

A horse starts pulling a man in a buggy.

A cat pushes a dog.

Representing Forces

Figure 3 In the first image, a short arrow in a downward direction shows that the bird is exerting a small downward force on the elephant. Draw arrows on the other images to represent the size and direction of the forces applied by the animals in action.

Infer Which image shows a force that causes a change in motion? Why does this force cause a change in motion, but the forces in the other images do not?

....

....

....

Literacy Connection

Draw Evidence Use an additional source to find out what a "normal" force is. Is a normal force a contact force or a noncontact force? What is the normal force on a single book on a shelf?

....

....

....

....

....

....

....

....

....

....

Types of Forces Forces can be classified as either contact forces or noncontact forces. Contact forces are those applied only when one object actually touches another. When you push a box across the floor, your push is a contact force because the force only exists while you touch the box. The box may be difficult to push because there is another contact force acting on the box in the opposite direction of your push. It is the force of friction between the box and the floor. **Friction** is a contact force that two surfaces exert on each other when they rub against each other. Friction between your feet and the sidewalk prevents you from slipping as you walk. Ice on the sidewalk greatly reduces that friction.

A noncontact force is a force applied to an object whether it touches the object or not. One noncontact force that you experience every day is **gravity**—a force that pulls objects toward each other as a result of their masses. The force of gravity pulls your body toward Earth. Magnetism and electrical forces are also noncontact forces. **Figure 4** shows examples of contact forces and noncontact forces.

☑ READING CHECK **Identify** What are three examples of noncontact forces?

....

....

Contact and Noncontact Forces

Figure 4 You use contact and noncontact forces daily. Complete the sentence in each caption by underlining either "contact" or "noncontact."

This girl exerts a force on the pedals of this bicycle, and friction between the tires and the road help to keep the bike from slipping. Both the force on the pedals and friction are (contact/noncontact) forces.

Even when your feet don't touch the ground, gravity pulls you toward Earth's surface. Gravity is a (contact/noncontact) force.

Balanced and Unbalanced Forces More than one force can act on an object. If two forces acting on an object are equal in strength and opposite in direction, they are balanced forces. A single book resting on a shelf has two forces acting on it. The downward force of gravity is equal in strength and opposite in direction to the upward force of the shelf on the book. The forces are balanced.

What happens when someone pulls the book off the shelf? The pull of the person removing the book and the friction between the shelf and the book also act in opposite directions. These two forces, however are not equal in strength. The pull is stronger than the friction. These forces are unbalanced.

When the forces on an object are unbalanced, there is a nonzero net force acting on the object. The **net force** on an object is the combination of all the forces acting on that object. If the forces act in the same direction, the net force is the sum of the forces. If the forces act in opposite directions, the net force is the difference in the strengths of those forces. If the net force turns out to be zero, the forces are balanced. Otherwise, the forces are unbalanced. A nonzero net force acting on an object causes a change in the object's motion.

INTERACTIVITY

Explore balanced and unbalanced forces in action.

Write About It! In your science notebook, describe two examples of how unbalanced forces help you in your everyday life.

Model It!

Forces in Tug-of-War

Figure 5 A tug-of-war competition demonstrates the effects of balanced and unbalanced forces on motion. The people on the left side of the rope are experiencing a force from the rope pulling them to the right. They are also experiencing friction from the ground pushing them to the left. The winning team is the team that experiences the greater force of friction.

Develop Models ✐ Draw more people on the left side of the rope to increase the force of friction experienced by this team. Add arrows to the model to represent the force from the rope and the force of friction on the people.

Effects of Net Force

In each diagram, two animals push on an apple. The forces of gravity and friction acting on the apple in each scenario does not change, so the forces that may cause a change will come from the animals.

Two chipmunks push on the apple in opposite directions with forces of equal strength. The forces on the apple are balanced. The motion and position of the apple do not change.

A chipmunk and a squirrel push on the apple in opposite directions with forces of different strengths. The forces on the apple are unbalanced. In this case, the strength of the net force on the apple is found by subtracting the strength of the smaller force from the strength of the larger force. The net force is in the same direction as the larger force.

A chipmunk and a squirrel push on the apple in the same direction. The forces on the apple are unbalanced. The net force on the apple is the sum of these forces. The apple will start moving to the right.

2N ➡ ⬅ 2N

2N ➡ ⬅ 6N

6N ➡
2N ➡

Net Force:

Net Force:

Net Force:

1. **Write an Inequality** For each set of forces, write one of these signs to compare the forces: =, >, <.

 2 N .... 2 N

 2 N .... 6 N

 8 N .... 0 N

2. **Apply Mathematical Concepts** 🖍 Label each diagram with the strength of the net force in newtons (N).

3. **Reason Quantitatively** In the center diagram, which direction will the apple start moving?

....

INTERACTIVITY

Check your understanding of net force in this interactivity.

✓ READING CHECK **Infer** A girl picks up a bag of apples that are at rest on the floor. How does the force the girl applies compare to the force of gravity acting on the apples?

....

....

....

MS-PS2-2

1. **Determine Differences** What is the difference between a contact force and a noncontact force?

   ....

   ....

   ....

2. **Apply Scientific Reasoning** A child is riding in a wagon. What reference point might have been used if an observer said the child was not moving?

   ....

   ....

   ....

3. **Calculate** Two children fight over a toy. One pulls with a force of 8 N to the right. The other pulls with a force of 6 N to the left. What is the strength and direction of the net force on the toy?

   ....

   ....

   ....

4. **Identify Criteria** A cow is grazing in a field. Under what conditions does the cow have relative motion?

   ....

   ....

   ....

   ....

5. **Synthesize Information** One man pushes on the front of a cart while another man pushes on the back of the cart. The cart begins to move forward. What are three things you know about these two applied forces?

   ....

   ....

   ....

   ....

   ....

   ....

Quest CHECK-IN

In this lesson, you learned about the motion of objects. You also learned about different types of forces and how these forces affect the movement of objects.

Identify What are the forces that act upon amusement park rides? Why is it important for engineers to understand how motion and forces affect the rides they design?

   ....

   ....

   ....

   ....

INTERACTIVITY

Define Criteria and Constraints

Go online to identify the problem, consider criteria and constraints, and develop a design for your prototype.

Speed, Velocity, and Acceleration

Guiding Questions

- How do you determine speed from calculations and distance-versus-time graphs?
- How is velocity related to speed and acceleration?
- How can you interpret graphs to determine acceleration?

Connections

Literacy Determine Conclusions

Math Solve Linear Equations

MS-PS2-2

HANDS-ON LAB

uInvestigate Experiment to find out how you can calculate your speed as you walk to your locker.

Vocabulary

speed
slope
velocity
acceleration

Academic Vocabulary

average
variable

Connect It !

 Draw an arrow to show the strength and direction of the force applied to the sled by the people pushing the sled.

Construct Explanations How does the snow help the sled move down the hill?

....

....

....

Describe How would you describe the difference in the motion of the sled from when the people first start pushing to when the sled is halfway down the hill?

....

....

Calculating Speed

You might describe the motion of the sled in **Figure 1** as slow when it starts moving and fast when it reaches the bottom of the hill. By using these words, you are describing the sled's speed. The **speed** of an object is the distance the object moves per unit of time. Speed is a type of rate. A rate tells you the amount of something that occurs or changes in one unit of time.

Distance Over Time To calculate the speed of an object, divide the distance the object travels by the amount of time it takes to travel that distance. This relationship can be written as an equation:

$$\text{Speed} = \frac{\text{Distance}}{\text{Time}}$$

Any unit that expresses distance over time is a unit of speed. Some examples of units of speed include kilometers per hour, miles per hour, and feet per minute. The SI unit for speed is meters per second, or m/s. For example, the sled might travel at a speed of 5 m/s near its starting point. This means that the sled travels a distance of 5 meters in 1 second. As it nears the bottom of the hill, the sled might be moving at a speed of about 15 m/s. This means that the sled travels a distance of 15 meters in 1 second. The greater the number of meters per second, the faster the speed at which the object is traveling.

INTERACTIVITY

Imagine what it would feel like to ride on a very fast amusement park ride.

Picking up Speed
Figure 1 Family members push each other on a sled from a stopped position at the top of the hill. As the sled glides down the hill, it moves faster and faster. This fast speed makes for a fun ride!

Investigate Experiment to find out how you can calculate your speed as you walk to your locker.

Academic Vocabulary

In math, you find an average by dividing the sum of values by the number of values given. How might you use the word *average* in a situation that does not involve math?

....

....

....

....

....

Instantaneous and Average Speeds

Think about the last time you rode in a car. Depending on road conditions and traffic, the speed of the vehicle varied. If you had looked at the speedometer for a moment in a traffic jam, it might have read 5 kilometers per hour. On the highway, at a particular instant, it might have read 88 kilometers per hour. The speed at a particular instant in time is called instantaneous speed.

Although you did not travel at the same speed for the whole trip, you did have an **average** speed throughout the trip. To calculate average speed, divide the total distance traveled by the total time. For example, suppose you drove a distance of 3 kilometers in 1 hour while in heavy traffic. Then, it took you 1 hour to drive 50 kilometers from one side of a city to the other. Finally, you traveled 211 kilometers on an interstate highway in 2 hours. The average speed of the car is the total distance traveled divided by the total time. In the equation below, you can see that your average speed on the road trip was 66 kilometers per hour.

Total distance = 3 km + 50 km + 211 km = 264 km

Total time = 1 h + 1 h + 2 h = 4 h

$$\text{Average speed} = \frac{264 \text{ km}}{4 \text{ h}} = 66 \text{ km/h}$$

✓ READING CHECK **Explain** How does instantaneous speed differ from average speed?

....

....

....

Average Speed

Figure 2 A racecar at the Daytona 500 zips around the track. It travels the first 80 kilometers in 0.4 hours. The next 114 kilometers take 0.6 hours. The following 80 kilometers take 0.4 hours. Calculate the racecar's average speed.

Calculating Speed From a Graph

The graph you see on this page is a distance-versus-time graph. Time is shown on the horizontal axis, or *x*-axis. Distance is shown on the vertical axis, or *y*-axis. A point on the line represents the distance an object has traveled during a given time period. The *x* value of the point is time, and the *y* value is distance. The angle of a line on a graph is called **slope**. The slope tells you how one **variable** changes in relation to the other variable in the graph. In other words, slope tells you the rate of change. You can calculate the slope of a line by dividing the rise by the run. The rise is the vertical difference between any two points on the line. The run is the horizontal difference between the same two points.

$$\text{Slope} = \frac{\text{Rise}}{\text{Run}}$$

The points in the graph below show a rise of 50 meters and a run of 2 seconds. To find the slope, divide 50 meters by 2 seconds. The slope is 25 meters per second. What do you notice about the units of slope? On a distance-versus-time graph, the units of the slope of the line are the same as the units for speed. Because speed is the rate that distance changes in relation to time, the slope of a distance-versus-time graph represents speed. The steeper the slope is, the greater the speed. A constant slope represents motion at constant speed.

INTERACTIVITY

Explore the speed of a space probe using a distance-versus-time graph.

Academic Vocabulary

A variable is a letter or symbol that represents a number that can change. Use *variable* as an adjective in a sentence. Explain what it means.

....

....

....

....

....

Math Toolbox

Using a Distance-Versus-Time Graph

The cheetah in this photograph is running at a constant speed. The graph shows the distance the cheetah moves and the time it takes the cheetah to move that distance.

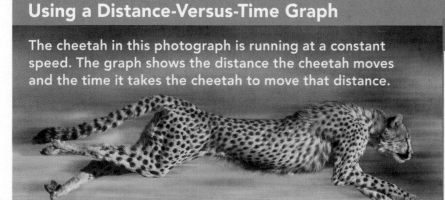

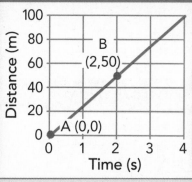

Cheetah's Motion

(graph: Distance (m) vs Time (s); points A (0,0) and B (2,50))

1. Calculate Mark two new points on the line. Use these points to calculate the slope.

....

....

2. Draw Conclusions What is the average speed of the cheetah?

....

3. Solve Linear Equations The graph of a straight line that goes through the origin can be represented by the equation, $y = mx$. This equation describes the relationship between the two variables *x* and *y*. In this equation, *m* represents the constant slope of the line. Use this equation to determine the distance the cheetah traveled in 4 seconds.

....

Velocity in Formations

Figure 3 Each member in this marching band must move at a specific velocity to be in the correct place in the formation. What part of velocity that is important for this formation is not shown by a distance-versus-time graph?

....

Apply Scientific Reasoning Do all of the members of the band have to move at the same velocity at all times? Explain your reasoning.

....
....
....
....
....
....
....

👆 **INTERACTIVITY**

Investigate the speed, velocity, and acceleration of a skydiver.

Describing Velocity

To describe an object's motion, you also need to know its direction. For example, suppose you hear that a thunderstorm is traveling at a speed of 25 km/h. Should you prepare for the storm? That depends on the direction in which the storm is moving. If it is traveling toward you, you might want to take cover. The speed at which an object travels in a given direction is called **velocity**. You know the velocity of a storm when you know that it is moving 25 km/h eastward.

In certain situations, describing the velocity of moving objects is important. For example, air traffic controllers must keep close track of the velocities of aircrafts. These velocities change as airplanes move overhead and on the runways. An error in determining a velocity, either in speed or in direction, could lead to a collision.

✓ **READING CHECK** **Determine Conclusions** How can understanding velocity help to prevent a mid-air collision?

....
....
....
....

Determining Acceleration

Speed and velocity are not the only ways to describe motion. Suppose you are a passenger in a car stopped at a red light. When the light changes to green, the driver steps on the gas pedal. As a result, the car speeds up, or accelerates. But acceleration means more than just speeding up. Scientists define **acceleration** as the rate at which velocity changes. A change in velocity can involve a change in speed, direction, or both. In science, when an object accelerates, it increases speed, decreases speed, or changes direction.

Change in Speed or Direction When the term *acceleration* is used, it means one of two things—any change in speed or any change in direction. A dog that starts running to chase a squirrel is accelerating. You accelerate when you start walking faster to get to class on time. When objects slow down, they are also accelerating. A car accelerates as it comes to a stop at a red light. A water skier accelerates as the boat slows down. A decrease in speed is sometimes called deceleration.

Even an object that is traveling at a constant speed is accelerating when it changes direction. Therefore, a car accelerates as it follows a gentle curve in the road or changes lanes. Runners accelerate as they round the curve in a track.

 VIDEO

Compare the speed and acceleration of different animals.

Model It

Acceleration

Figure 4 This image shows a basketball player shooting a ball.

1. **Develop Models** ✏️ Label the two sections of the path to identify where the ball increases speed and decreases speed.

2. **Use Models** Besides the labels for changing speed, what is another way that you can tell from this model that the ball is accelerating?

....

....

....

Acceleration in Racing

Figure 5 The pictures show different ways acceleration occurs in a race. Label each image as either increasing speed, decreasing speed, or changing direction.

Starting Line

Curve

Finish Line

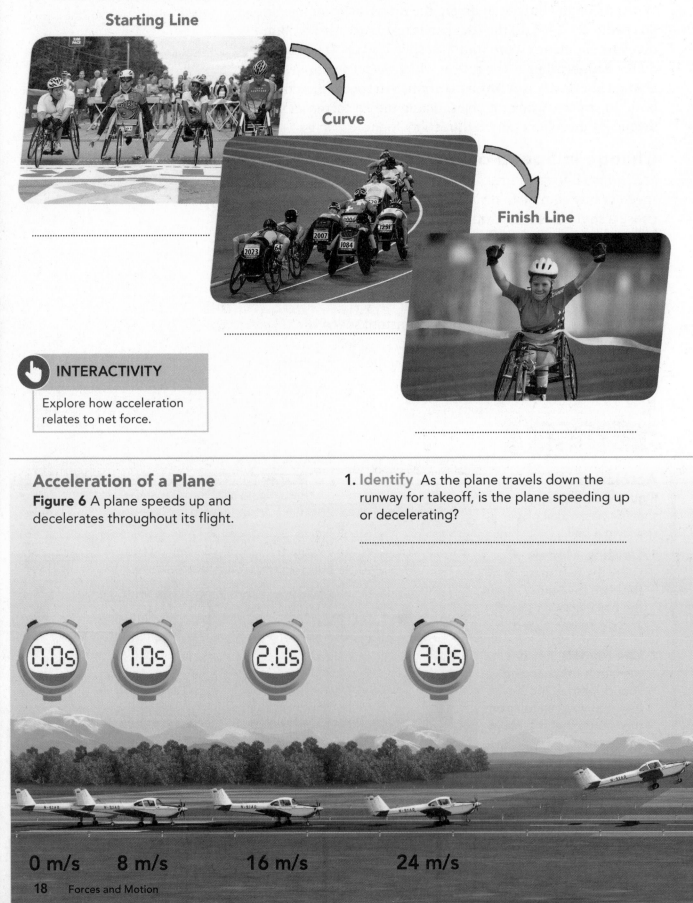

👆 **INTERACTIVITY**

Explore how acceleration relates to net force.

Acceleration of a Plane

Figure 6 A plane speeds up and decelerates throughout its flight.

1. Identify As the plane travels down the runway for takeoff, is the plane speeding up or decelerating?

| 0.0s | 1.0s | 2.0s | 3.0s |

| 0 m/s | 8 m/s | 16 m/s | 24 m/s |

Calculating Acceleration If an object is not changing direction, you can describe its acceleration as the rate at which its speed changes. To determine the acceleration of an object moving in a straight line, you calculate the change in speed per unit of time. This is summarized by the following equation:

$$\text{Acceleration} = \frac{\text{Final speed} - \text{Initial speed}}{\text{Time}}$$

Since speed is measured in meters per second (m/s) and time is measured in seconds, acceleration is meters per second per second, or m/s^2. This unit is the SI unit for acceleration.

To understand acceleration, imagine a small airplane moving down a runway, preparing for takeoff. **Figure 6** shows the airplane's speed after each second of its acceleration. To calculate the acceleration of the airplane during takeoff, you must first subtract the initial speed of 0 m/s from its final speed of 24 m/s. Then divide the change in speed by the time, 3 seconds.

$$\text{Acceleration} = \frac{24 \text{ m/s} - 0 \text{ m/s}}{3 \text{ s}}$$

$$\text{Acceleration} = 8 \text{ m/s}^2$$

The airplane accelerates at a rate of 8 m/s^2. This means that the airplane's speed increases by 8 m/s every second. Notice in **Figure 6** that after each second of travel during takeoff, the airplane's speed is 8 m/s greater than its speed in the previous second.

2. **Calculate** On landing, the plane touches the runway with a speed of 65 m/s. The figure shows the speed of the plane after 1 second. Calculate the acceleration of the plane during its landing.

....

....

3. **Translate Information** What does a negative value for acceleration mean here?

....

....

65 m/s

60 m/s

Graphing Acceleration Suppose you bike down a long, steep hill. At the top of the hill, your speed is 0 m/s. As you start down the hill, your speed increases. Each second, you move at a greater speed and travel a greater distance than the second before. During the five seconds it takes you to reach the bottom of the hill, you are accelerating. Use the data provided in **Figure 7** to graph and analyze your motion on the accelerating bike.

✅ **READING CHECK** **Summarize** How are the speed, velocity, and acceleration of a moving object related?

....

....

....

0s

1s

2s

3s

4s

5s

Graphing Acceleration

Figure 7 This table lists the distance the bike travels from the top of the hill and the speed of the bike at each second as it accelerates down the hill.

Time (s)	Distance (m)	Speed (m/s)
0	0	0
1	1	2
2	4	4
3	9	6
4	16	8
5	25	10

1. **Create a Graph** 🖉 Use the data in the table to create a distance-versus-time graph on the first grid. Plot distance on the vertical axis and time on the horizontal axis.

2. **Create a Graph** 🖉 On the second grid, create a speed-versus-time graph. Plot speed on the vertical axis and time on the horizontal axis.

3. **Apply Concepts** Compare the distance-versus-time graph in this figure to the distance-versus-time graph in the Math Toolbox in this lesson. Why does one graph have a straight line, while the other graph has a curved line?

....

....

....

....

1. Relate Change What three changes in motion show that an object is accelerating?

....

....

2. Calculate What is the average speed of a train that covers 80 km in 1 h, 200 km in 2 h, and 420 km in 4 h?

....

....

....

3. Evaluate Your Claim A ball is pushed from a stop and rolls 6 m in 2 s. Student A says the average speed of the ball is 3 m/s. Student B says the average speed of the ball is 1.5 m/s^2. Which student is correct? Explain your answer.

....

....

....

....

....

4. Interpret Data A student graphed distance versus time for an object that moves 14 m every 2 s. What is the slope of the line on the graph? Explain.

....

....

....

....

5. Apply Scientific Reasoning If the line on a distance-versus-time graph and the line on a speed-versus-time graph are both straight lines going through the origin, can the two graphs be displaying the motion of the same object? Explain.

....

....

....

....

....

....

Quest CHECK-IN

In this lesson, you learned how motion can be described by speed, velocity, and acceleration. You also learned how to use mathematical formulas to calculate and graph average speed and acceleration.

Use Models How might you use a model of a bumper car to determine how speed and acceleration affect the motion of the car? What materials might you use?

....

....

....

....

HANDS-ON LAB

Mass, Speed, and Colliding Cars

Go online to download the lab worksheet. Learn about the features of bumper cars that affect acceleration, including positive acceleration, deceleration, and changes in direction. Brainstorm additional features that might affect speed in bumper cars.

MS-PS2-2

FINDING YOUR WAY

WITH GPS

Before the advent of the global positioning system (GPS), people had two choices if they were traveling in an unfamiliar area. They could either use a map or find someone to ask for directions.

Today, almost everyone relies on GPS, whether in car navigation systems or on smartphones and tablets. But what exactly is GPS, and how does it provide data about a moving object's location and speed?

The heart of this system is a network of more than 24 satellites orbiting Earth. These satellites form a "cloud" around the planet so that at least four of them are in the sky at any given place and time. System engineers monitor each satellite to keep careful track of its position.

How GPS Works
Nearby satellites send radio signals to the GPS device, and the device calculates its position based on its distance from those satellites. Four satellites are needed for a GPS to calculate its latitude, longitude, and altitude with accuracy. If fewer satellites are used, only a relative position of the GPS device can be determined, not an exact location.

How GPS WORKS

Satellite

1 Each satellite transmits a radio signal in the form of electromagnetic waves. The signal contains data about the satellite's precise location and the time the signal was sent.

2 The radio signal travels toward Earth at the speed of light.

3 A GPS device receives the signals from the satellites overhead. The device uses the speed of light and the time it takes for the signal to reach the receiver to calculate its distance from each satellite. Using these distances, the device calculates its exact position.

DISTANCE

GPS Receiver

Use the text and the diagram to answer the following questions.

1. Use Models How does the GPS determine its distance from each satellite?

2. Calculate A radio signal from a GPS satellite takes only about 0.067 seconds to reach a GPS receiver. If the speed of light is about 300,000 km/s, then approximately how far away is the receiver from the satellite? Show your calculations.

3. Apply Scientific Reasoning Why is it necessary for engineers to know the precise location of each GPS satellite in the system?

4. Construct Explanations Explain how a GPS device can determine the speed at which it is moving. Provide a real-world example to support your response.

23

Newton's Laws of Motion

Guiding Questions

- How do Newton's laws of motion describe when and how objects move?
- How do an object's mass and the forces acting upon an object affect its motion?
- What are action and reaction forces, and how do they impact an object's motion?

Connections

Literacy Use Information

Math Evaluate Expressions

MS-PS2-2

HANDS-ON LAB

uInvestigate Use Newton's third law to design a vehicle that moves forward by pushing backward.

Vocabulary

inertia

Academic Vocabulary

derived

Connect It!

✏️ **A hockey player hits a puck that was at rest on the ice. Mark an X on the point in the image where the hockey player first applied a net force to the puck.**

Cause and Effect How did the motion of the puck change as a result of being hit?

....

....

Infer After being hit, the puck travels along the ice at a constant speed. What might cause its motion to change?

....

....

Newton's First Law of Motion

If you were watching an ice-hockey game, you would be surprised if a puck that was sitting still suddenly started moving without being hit. You would also be surprised if a moving puck suddenly stopped in the middle of the ice. Your surprise would be the result of knowing that a net force must act upon an object to cause a change in motion. This natural phenomenon that you observe in the world demonstrates Newton's first law of motion.

Newton's first law of motion states that an object at rest will remain at rest unless acted upon by a nonzero net force. Therefore, a hockey puck that is sitting still will remain at rest unless a player hits it, applying a net force. This law also states that an object moving at a constant velocity will continue moving at a constant velocity unless acted upon by a nonzero net force. You can see this law in action when a hockey puck slides in a straight line across the ice. The motion remains constant until it hits something like the net of the goal or another hockey stick.

A simple statement of Newton's first law of motion is that if an object is not moving, it will not start moving until a net force acts on it. If an object is moving, it will continue at a constant velocity until a net force acts to change its speed or its direction. If there is a net force acting on an object, it will accelerate.

Literacy Connection

Use Information As you read these pages, underline information you can use to define Newton's first law.

INTERACTIVITY

Explore what causes a ball to stop rolling.

Speeding Up

Figure 1 Just a moment ago, the puck was at rest on the ice. The net force that the player applied to the puck caused the puck to accelerate.

Mass and Inertia

Figure 2 Suppose each of these women wants to move the dog off of her lap.

Which dog has less inertia? ....

Which dog is harder to move?

....

Inertia Resistance to change in motion is called **inertia**. So Newton's first law is also called the law of inertia. Inertia explains many common events, including why seat belts and air bags are used in vehicles. If you are riding in a moving car, you are moving at the same speed the car is moving. When brakes apply a force to the car, the car decelerates. The brakes did not apply a force to you, however, so inertia keeps you moving forward at the same speed and direction you were going before the car decelerated. A force, such as the pull of a seat belt, is needed to pull you back.

Inertia and Mass Which object—you or the car—is harder to stop? Based on your own experience, you can probably figure out that the car is harder to stop. That is because it has more mass. The more massive object has a greater inertia, as in **Figure 2.**

Once Newton had described the connection between inertia and mass, he next figured out how to find the acceleration of an object when a force acted on it.

☑ **READING CHECK** **Summarize** How does mass relate to inertia?

....

....

Newton's Second Law of Motion

Newton's first law stated that inertia exists for an object. Newton then explained that an object's mass directly affects how much force is needed to accelerate the object.

Changes in Acceleration and Mass Suppose that you apply a constant net force on an object. How does changing the mass of the object affect its acceleration? You can see this with a horse-drawn sleigh, shown in **Figure 3**. The horses provide a steady force. If the sleigh is empty, it will accelerate quickly when the horses pull on it. If the sleigh is full of people, it has a greater inertia and will accelerate slowly. The acceleration of the sleigh will change depending on the mass of the load it carries. Newton understood these relationships and found a way to represent them mathematically.

Calculating Force Newton's second law of motion states that the size and direction of a net force equals the mass times the acceleration. The net force will have the same direction as the acceleration. This relationship can be written as follows:

$$\text{Net force} = \text{Mass} \times \text{Acceleration}$$

If the net force and mass are known, the resulting acceleration can be **derived** by using this equation:

$$\text{Acceleration} = \frac{\text{Net force}}{\text{Mass}}$$

Academic Vocabulary
Read the sentence in which the word *derived* is used, and infer its meaning.

....

....

....

....

Newton's Second Law
Figure 3 The force applied by these two horses pulls the sleigh and the people it contains. This sleigh can contain up to 12 people.

1. **Reason Quantitatively** How might you change the number of people to increase the sleigh's acceleration?

....

....

....

2. **Apply Scientific Reasoning** How might you change the number of people to decrease the sleigh's acceleration?

....

....

....

READING CHECK

Use Information A dog walks along the ground. If the dog applies an action force on the ground, what is the reaction force?

....

....

....

Detecting Forces and Motion Some results of action-reaction forces are easily observed. If you were the skateboarder in **Figure 4**, you could feel the force of the ground on your foot. You could see and feel the skateboard accelerate. If you drop your pen, gravity pulls the pen downward and you can see it fall.

But some changes caused by action-reaction forces are not as easily detected. When you drop your pen, the pen pulls Earth upward with an equal and opposite reaction force, according to Newton's third law. You see the pen fall, but you don't see Earth accelerate toward the pen. Remember Newton's second law. If mass increases and force stays the same, acceleration decreases. The same force acts on both Earth and your pen. Because Earth has such a large mass, its acceleration is so small that you don't notice it.

Balanced and Action-Reaction Forces You have learned that two equal forces acting in opposite directions on an object balance each other and produce no change in motion. So why aren't the action-reaction forces in Newton's third law of motion balanced as well? In order for forces to balance, they must act on the same object. Action-reaction forces are not balanced because they act on different objects. When a hockey player hits a puck with his stick, the action force is the force of the stick on the puck. The reaction force is the force of the puck on the stick. So one force acts on the puck, while the other acts on the stick. The puck has a much smaller mass than the player and his stick, so you see the puck accelerate. See how other action-reaction forces act on different objects in **Figure 5**.

Understanding Action-Reaction

Figure 5 🖉 Action-reaction forces are applied to different objects. The action and reaction forces acting on a soccer player, a soccer ball, and the ground are shown with arrows. Finish labeling the forces to describe how they are being applied.

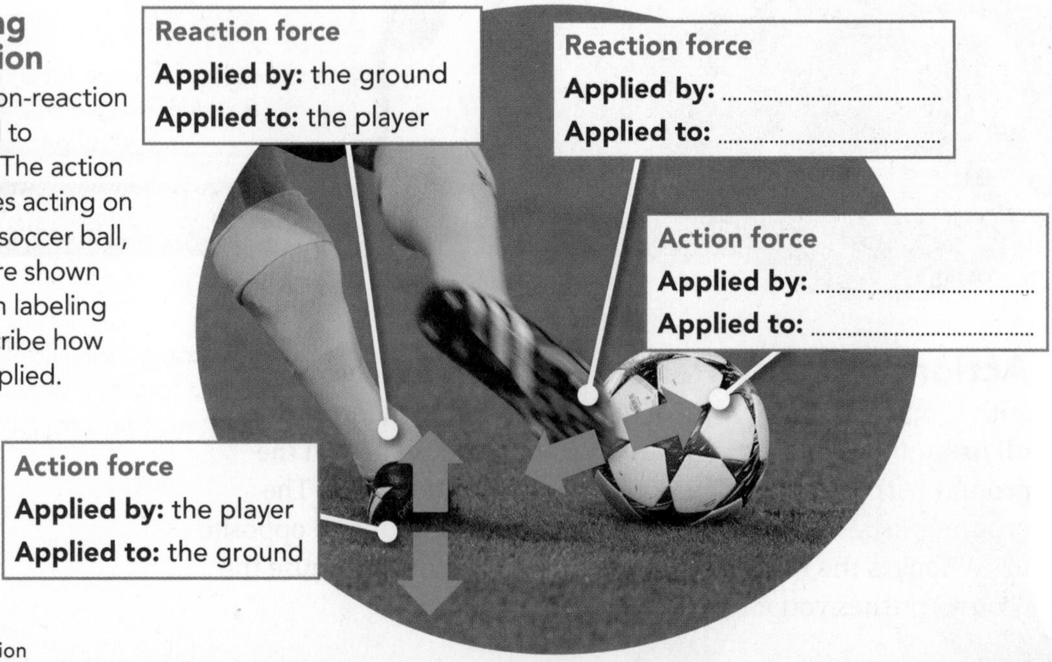

Reaction force
Applied by: the ground
Applied to: the player

Reaction force
Applied by: ....
Applied to: ....

Action force
Applied by: ....
Applied to: ....

Action force
Applied by: the player
Applied to: the ground

Applying Newton's Laws

Kirsten has a parakeet that likes to sit on a swing. Sometimes the bird makes the swing move back and forth.

Ask Questions You want to investigate the bird and his swing and how they relate to Newton's laws of motion. List at least two questions you might ask.

....

....

Newton's Laws Together When you have a situation involving force, acceleration, and mass, it usually involves two or even all three of Newton's laws! Look at **Figure 6** to see how Newton's laws apply to an amusement park ride.

Reflect Describe how Newton's laws of motion are involved in an activity in your daily life.

Newton's First Law:	Newton's Second Law:	Newton's Third Law:

Newton's Laws

Figure 6 ✏ In each space provided, give an example of a way that one of Newton's laws is shown in this amusement park ride.

☑ LESSON 3 Check

MS-PS2-2

1. **Communicate** In your own words, what is Newton's second law of motion?

....

....

....

....

2. **Apply Concepts** What is inertia? Use an example in your description.

....

....

....

3. **Integrate Information** What is the difference between balanced forces and action-reaction forces?

....

....

....

....

4. **Explain Phenomena** You push on a door and it opens. Explain what happens in terms of action-reaction forces.

....

....

....

....

....

....

5. **Calculate** A 12-N net force acts on a 4-kg jug of water. What is the resulting acceleration of the jug? Show your calculations.

....

....

....

Quest CHECK-IN

In this lesson, you learned how Newton's laws explain the motions of moving objects and how mass affects acceleration. You also learned that every action has an equal and opposite reaction.

Apply Concepts How would Newton's laws of motion relate to the movement of bumper cars? How might the mass of the riders and the speed of the cars affect this movement?

....

....

....

....

....

👆 INTERACTIVITY

Apply Newton's Laws of Motion

Go online to learn about how action-reaction forces affect the movement of vehicles in collisions. Then brainstorm how these forces would affect bumper cars.

littleBits
CHALLENGE

GENERATING ENERGY
from Potholes

👆 **INTERACTIVITY**

Explore how Newton's laws can be used to design more fuel-efficient vehicles.

Traveling in a car over uneven road surfaces and potholes can make for a bouncy ride. How can you capture the energy generated by that bouncing motion? You engineer it!

The Challenge: To convert the motion of a car into electrical energy.

Phenomenon When a car travels down the road, the car exerts an action force on the road, and the road exerts a reaction force on the wheels of the car. A bumpy road occasionally exerts a stronger force than a smooth road, which means an uncomfortable ride for passengers. That's where shock absorbers come in. Shock absorbers are part of a car's suspension system, and they cause the body of the car to react slowly to bumps. This decreases the force exerted on a car by the road.

With traditional shock absorbers, the energy that is absorbed is then released as heat. Auto engineers have now found a way to use their understanding of the Law of Conservation of Energy to harness this energy. They have developed electromechanical shock absorbers that use a lever arm to capture the up-and-down motion of the wheels. A device called an alternator transforms this kinetic energy into electricity. The engineers hope that this electrical energy can be used to increase the fuel efficiency of cars.

With electromechanical shock absorbers, the energy generated by bumps and potholes can be transformed into electrical energy.

DESIGN CHALLENGE Can you build a shock absorber? Go to the Engineering Design Notebook to find out!

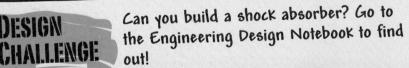

(4) Friction and Gravitational Interactions

Guiding Questions

- What factors affect the different types of friction?
- What factors affect gravity?
- How are gravity and friction related to motion and energy?

Connections

Literacy Write Arguments

Math Analyze Relationships

MS-PS2-4, MS-PS3-2

HANDS-ON LAB

иInvestigate Explore how friction is affected by different surfaces, and investigate how the force of friction affects the motion of objects.

Vocabulary

weight

Academic Vocabulary

associate

Connect It

✏️ **Circle two areas that show what causes the bike to slow down.**

Identify What force is responsible for stopping the bike?

....

Classify Is this force a contact or noncontact force? Explain.

....

....

....

Factors That Affect Friction

Recall that the force two surfaces exert on each other when they rub against each other is the contact force called friction. For example, if you slide a book across a table, the surface of the book rubs against the surface of the table. The resulting force is friction. This force acts in a direction opposite to the motion of the book and eventually stops the book.

Two Factors Both the types of surfaces involved and how hard the surfaces are pushed together affect the friction between two surfaces. The bicyclist in **Figure 1** is using friction to slow his bicycle. One place where friction occurs on the bicycle is between the tires and the ground. Have you ever examined the surface of a tire? The tread on the tire results in more friction between the tire and the ground. A tire on a mountain bike has more tread on it than a regular bike tire, so a lot of friction is produced between a mountain bike tire and the ground. In general, smoother surfaces produce less friction than rougher surfaces.

In this instance, friction also occurs between the brake pads and the wheels. This friction prevents the tire from turning. The harder the bicyclist applies the brakes, the more quickly the bike will come to a stop. Friction increases as surfaces push harder against each other.

Friction acts in a direction opposite to the direction of the object's motion. Without friction or some other force acting in the opposite direction, a moving object will not stop until it strikes another object.

INTERACTIVITY

Describe your experiences riding a bicycle on different surfaces.

Skidding to a Stop
Figure 1 This mountain biker applies his brakes and skids to slow down.

Types of Friction
Use **Figure 2** to find out more about four different types of friction.

☑ READING CHECK **Write Arguments** How can you be sure that the skater leaping through the air is moving faster than the one speeding along the ground?

....

....

Friction in a Skatepark

Figure 2 🖊 Add labels to three other skaters in the figure to identify the type of friction that is opposing their motion. Then, for each type of friction described, identify another example of that type of friction.

Rolling Friction

When an object rolls across a surface, rolling friction occurs. Rolling friction is just sliding friction between two very smooth surfaces (the axle and the bearing of wheels, for example). If similar materials are used, rolling friction is much easier to overcome than sliding friction. That's why a skateboard with wheels that turn is easy to push on a sidewalk. It would be more difficult to push a skateboard if it had no wheels.

Another example:

....

Sliding Friction

Sliding friction occurs when two solid surfaces slide across each other. Sliding friction is what makes moving objects slow down and stop. Without sliding friction, a skater who falls would skid along the ground until he hit a wall!

Another example:

....

HANDS-ON LAB

⊔Investigate Explore how friction is affected by different surfaces, and investigate how the force of friction affects the motion of objects.

Static Friction

Static friction acts on objects when they are resting on a surface. The skater trying to push the ramp is experiencing the force of static friction. Think about trying to push a couch across the room. If you don't push hard enough, the couch won't move. The force that's keeping the couch from moving is static friction between the couch and the floor. If you get some friends to help you push hard enough to overcome static friction, the couch starts moving and there is no more static friction. At that point, there is sliding friction.

Another example:

....

Fluid Friction

Fluids, such as water and air, flow easily. Fluid friction occurs when a solid object moves through a fluid. Fluid friction from your contact with water acts on your body when you swim. It also acts on a skater's body when he does a trick in mid-air. When an object moves through the air, the fluid friction acting on the object is often referred to as air resistance. Fluid friction is typically easier to overcome than sliding friction.

Another example:

....

Universal Gravitation

Figure 3 How does the gravitational attraction between these people compare to the gravitational attraction between the people and Earth?

....

....

▶ **VIDEO**

Explore why the moon is able to circle Earth without falling toward it.

☑ READING CHECK

Summarize What is the law of universal gravitation?

....

....

....

....

Factors That Affect Gravity

While friction is an example of a contact force, gravity is an example on a non-contact force. Remember that gravity is a force that pulls objects toward each other. How is gravity experienced on Earth? You could name many examples. A basketball player shoots a ball toward the basket, and the ball falls toward Earth. Rain falls from the sky to Earth. We are so familiar with objects falling that we may not think much about why they fall. One person who thought about this was Sir Isaac Newton. He concluded that a force called gravity acts to pull objects straight down toward the center of Earth.

Universal Gravitation Newton realized that gravity acts everywhere in the universe, not just on Earth. It is the force that causes the tides in Earth's ocean and keeps all the planets in our solar system orbiting around the sun. On Earth, gravity is the force that makes the jumpers in **Figure 3** fall toward the water.

Newton's realization is now called the law of universal gravitation. This law states that the force of gravity acts between all objects in the universe that have mass. So, any two objects in the universe that have mass attract each other. You are attracted not only to Earth but also to your school desk, the other planets in the solar system, and the most distant star you can see. Earth and the objects around you are attracted to you as well. You can clearly see the gravitational effect of Earth on an object. However, you do not notice the attraction between objects on Earth because these forces are extremely small compared to the attraction between the objects and Earth itself.

Factors Affecting Gravity

What factors control the strength of the gravitational force between two objects? These factors are the mass of each object and the distance between them.

The more mass an object has, the greater the gravitational force between it and other objects. Earth's gravitational force on nearby objects is strong because the mass of Earth is so large. Gravitational force also depends on the distance between the objects' centers. As distance increases, gravitational force decreases. What happens when you drop your cell phone? You see your cell phone fall to Earth because Earth and your cell phone are close together. If your cell phone were on the moon, Earth would not exert a visible gravitational attraction to it because Earth and the phone would be so far apart. The phone would be visibly attracted to the moon instead.

Weight and Mass

Mass is sometimes confused with weight. Mass is a measure of the amount of matter in an object. **Weight** is a measure of the force of gravity on an object. Since weight is a measure of force, the SI unit of weight is a newton (N). If you know the mass of an object in kilograms, you can calculate its weight on Earth using Newton's second law. The acceleration due to gravity at Earth's surface is 9.8 m/s². The force is the weight of the object.

$$\text{Net force} = \text{Mass} \times \text{Acceleration}$$

When you stand on a bathroom scale, it displays your weight—the gravitational force that Earth is exerting on you. On Earth, 1 pound equals 4.45 newtons. If you could stand on the surface of Jupiter, which has a mass around 300 times the mass of Earth, your mass would remain the same, but your weight would increase. This is because the gravitational force exerted on you is greater on Jupiter than on Earth.

Describing g-Forces

Figure 4 A lowercase g is used as the symbol for acceleration due to gravity at Earth's surface (9.8 m/s²). This symbol is used in the field of space engineering, where acceleration is often measured in "g"s. Engineers must design space shuttles considering the acceleration and forces that the crew and the shuttle itself would experience during flight.

INTERACTIVITY

Investigate how gravity affects falling objects.

Literacy Connection

Write Arguments Write an argument supported by evidence that explains why the pencil and notebook resting on your desk are not being pulled together by the force of gravity between them.

....

....

....

....

....

....

☑ LESSON 4 Check

1. Synthesize Information What is the difference between weight and mass?

....

....

....

....

2. Identify Snow has been lying on a mountainside. Suddenly, it starts to move down the mountain. Which types of friction are observed in this avalanche? Where does each type occur?

....

....

....

....

....

3. Apply Scientific Reasoning Give a real-life example of fluid friction.

....

....

....

....

4. Explain Phenomena A 4-kg ball is 2 cm away from one 1-kg ball and 6 cm away from another 1-kg ball. Use the relationships among the balls to describe two factors that affect gravity. Also explain why the balls do not move toward each other unless acted upon by another force.

....

....

....

....

....

....

....

....

....

5. Construct Explanations Rather than push a heavy box from one room to another, a worker chooses to place the box on a wheeled cart. In terms of friction, explain why moving the box on the wheeled cart is easier than pushing.

....

....

....

....

....

 CHECK-IN

In this lesson, you learned how different types of friction affect the movement of objects. You also learned about universal gravitation and how this scientific law applies to objects on Earth and elsewhere in the universe.

Evaluate How might friction affect the movement of bumper cars? What role does gravity play in how bumper cars move? How might you use these concepts to make bumper cars safer?

....

....

....

....

HANDS-ON LAB

Bumper Cars, Bumper Solutions

Go online to download the worksheet for this lab. Learn how friction and gravity affect vehicles on different surfaces. Then brainstorm how these factors influence the speed and direction of bumper cars.

MS-PS2-2

Spacetime Curvature and Gravitational Waves

How does mass cause objects to attract one another? The famous scientist Albert Einstein explored this question and came up with a revolutionary theory of gravity. It explains the existence of gravitational waves, while Newton's theory could not!

In Einstein's theory, space and time are not separate from one another. They make up a four-dimensional fabric that can warp and curve. Imagine that a ball is placed on a puffy comforter. The ball sinks into the comforter so that the comforter curves around it. Objects with mass sit in spacetime in a similar way. If you roll a marble past the ball, the marble circles around the ball. The marble gets caught in a groove created by the ball. That's basically how gravity works—objects attract one another by falling into grooves of spacetime.

Now, add acceleration into the picture, and you get ripples in the fabric of spacetime! For example, when two stars circle each other, they accelerate faster and faster. This acceleration produces ripples in spacetime similar to ripples of water on a pond.

Scientists detected gravitational waves for the first time on September 14, 2015. By detecting gravitational waves, we can learn about events all around the universe, such as black holes colliding!

MY DISCOVERY

Check out magazine articles on gravitational waves at your local library.

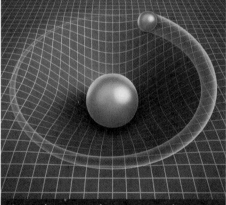

Any object with mass, such as Earth, causes the fabric of spacetime to curve. The result of this curvature is gravitational attraction.

As these stars accelerate, they create ripples in spacetime called gravitational waves.

Describing Motion and Force

MS-PS2-2

1. A girl pushes on the classroom door to open it. Which two terms accurately describe the net force acting on the door?
A. contact and balanced
B. contact and unbalanced
C. noncontact and balanced
D. noncontact and unbalanced

2. A dog is pulling on a leash while walking down the sidewalk. What frame of reference would indicate that the dog is not moving?
A. A nearby building   B. A tree
C. The leash   D. The sidewalk

3. Two dogs pull on a rope. One dog pulls with a force of 5 N to the left, and the other dog pulls with a force of 3 N to the right. What is the result?
A. The rope remains in place.
B. The rope moves to the left.
C. The rope moves to the right.
D. The rope has a balanced force applied to it.

4. Develop Models Using pictures, labels, and arrows, model a box that has two forces acting on it, 12 N to the right and 4 N to the left. Also show the net force on the box.

2 **Speed, Velocity, and Acceleration**

MS-PS2-2

5. A bus driver drove from Philadelphia to Washington D.C. He drove the first 100 km in 2 hours, the next 55 km in 1 hour, and the final 75 km in 2 hours. What is the average speed of the bus throughout the trip?
A. 46 km/h
B. 50 km/h
C. 77 km/h
D. 81 km/h

6. Which statement about acceleration is always true?
A. The unit m/s is the SI unit of acceleration.
B. For objects to accelerate, they must speed up.
C. Either a change in speed or a change in direction causes acceleration.
D. Both speed and direction must change for acceleration to occur.

7. A cross-country runner runs 4 km in 15 minutes. What can you calculate using this information?
A. acceleration
B. force
C. speed
D. velocity

8. You can find the speed on a distance-versus-time graph by finding the .... of the line.

9. Identify Criteria A woman is taking a walk, moving at a rate of 80 m/min. What additional information would you need to determine her velocity?

....

....

....

3 **Newton's Laws of Motion**

MS-PS2-2

10. A soccer player kicks a ball. Which of the following describes the reaction force to this kick?
A. friction between the ball and the foot
B. friction between the ball and the ground
C. force applied to the ground by the foot
D. force applied to the foot by the ball

11. Which term describes resistance to change in motion?
A. Acceleration
B. Inertia
C. Net force
D. Velocity

12. The acceleration of a baseball after it is hit by a bat depends on the mass of the ball and the net force on the ball. This example best illustrates what law?
A. Newton's first law of motion
B. Newton's second law of motion
C. Newton's third law of motion
D. Newton's law of universal gravitation

13. Integrate Information Describe how each of Newton's laws may be observable during a car trip.

....

....

....

....

....

....

....

....

4 **Friction and Gravitational Interactions**

MS-PS2-4, MS-PS3-2

14. When is there static friction between your desk chair and the floor?
A. when the chair sits still
B. when the chair falls to the floor
C. when you lift the chair
D. when you slide your chair under your desk

15. The amount of matter an object contains is ...., and the force of gravity on that matter is ....

16. A group of skydivers are riding in a helicopter up to the spot from which they will jump. As they ride upward, their gravitational potential energy _____.
A. decreases
B. remains constant
C. increases
D. changes to kinetic energy

17. Apply Concepts Using examples, explain how each of the four types of friction are present during lunch time in the school cafeteria.

....

....

....

....

....

....

....

....

....

45

MS-PS2-1, MS-PS2-2,
MS-PS2-4

Evidence-Based Assessment

In 2005, NASA sent a robotic spacecraft called DART to a satellite that was orbiting Earth. DART was supposed to demonstrate that it could move around the satellite and communicate with it, without a human on board. The spacecraft was supposed to come close to the satellite without actually touching it.

Here is how the DART system works: The spacecraft's navigation system estimates its position and speed. Then, commands are sent to the thrusters to keep the spacecraft along its intended path. Force from the thrusters causes a change in motion. If the GPS system communicates incorrect navigation data to the spacecraft, then it will travel incorrectly and use up its fuel.

DART made it into space, but then its navigation system failed, providing incorrect data on its position and speed. This failure caused DART to bump into the satellite. The force of the collision changed the motion of the satellite. Luckily it remained in orbit around Earth, but the mission was deemed a failure. Though NASA has had many successes, the science and engineering work involved with space exploration is extremely complex, and sometimes even the best-planned projects fail.

The diagram below shows the relative positions of DART, and the satellite before the collision.

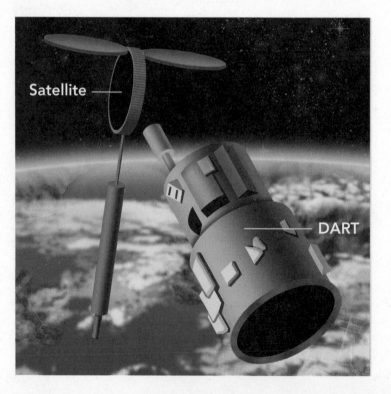

1. **Apply Scientific Reasoning** If the satellite had less mass, but the force of the collision was the same, then the collision would have
   A. caused the satellite to accelerate more quickly.
   B. caused the satellite to accelerate more slowly.
   C. caused the satellite to accelerate at the same rate.
   D. had no effect on the satellite's original motion.

2. **Cite Evidence** Did DART apply a balanced or unbalanced force to the satellite during the collision? What evidence supports your answer?

   ....
   ....
   ....
   ....
   ....

3. **Draw Comparative Inferences** Describe the action-reaction forces during the collision between DART and the satellite.

   ....
   ....
   ....
   ....

4. **Distinguish Relationships** Which do you think is stronger—the gravitational attraction between DART and Earth, or the gravitational attraction between DART and the satellite? Explain your answer.

   ....
   ....
   ....
   ....
   ....

5. **Synthesize Information** What labels and symbols could you add to an image to represent the forces acting on DART and the satellite during the collision? Describe what you would draw and write.

   ....
   ....
   ....
   ....
   ....
   ....
   ....
   ....
   ....

Quest FINDINGS

Complete the Quest!

Phenomenon Design a way to present your new bumper car design and the results of your testing to your class. Be sure to include how you applied Newton's third law of motion to your design.

Synthesize Information Bumper cars have safety features to protect both the riders and the cars themselves. These features are built around how forces and the laws of motion affect the movement of the cars. What is another example of how forces and laws of motion impact your safety in your daily life?

   ....
   ....
   ....

👆 **INTERACTIVITY**

Reflect on Your Bumper Car Solution

Stopping on a Dime

How can you **design a basketball court** so that players don't run into band members and other spectators near the court lines?

Background

Phenomenon Imagine your school is hosting a championship basketball game, and the school band will be playing at the game. The band director wants the band to set up its instruments very close to the out-of-bounds line of the basketball court, so that the band will be front and center during the game. Some people at the school, however, have raised concerns about this plan. They feel that having band members so close to the court is unsafe because the members might be hit by players running off the court.

You and some of your fellow science students have been asked to design and conduct an experiment to determine whether or not the band director's plan is safe for both the band members and the players. In this experiment, you will investigate how time, distance, and average speed relate to changes in motion, and you will apply these concepts to the players on the basketball court.

Materials

(per group)

- tape measure
- 2 stopwatches or watches with second hands

Design Your Investigation

To model the basketball players running off the court, you will determine the speed of someone running a distance of 10 meters. Your will also determine how far it takes the runner to come to a complete stop after hitting the 10-meter mark. Discuss with your group how you will design and conduct the investigation. As you plan, consider the following questions with your group:

HANDS-ON LAB

uDemonstrate Go online for a downloadable worksheet of this lab.

1. What three properties of the players in motion do you need to consider?

2. What do you need to know to calculate the speed of a runner?

3. What tests will you perform?

4. How many trials of each test will you perform?

5. What type of data will you be collecting? How will you collect, record, and organize your data?

6. What evidence will you need to present after your investigation?

7. How will you present your evidence to communicate your results effectively?

Write your plan in the space provided on the next page. After getting your teacher's approval, conduct your investigation. Record the data you collect in your group data table.

Procedure

....
....
....
....
....
....
....
....
....
....

Data Table

Speed (m/s)

Stopping Distance (m)

Analyze and Interpret Data

1. **Characterize Data** Why was it important to carry out the steps of your procedure multiple times with each participant?

....

....

....

....

2. **Apply Concepts** How are unbalanced forces at work when a runner attempts to stop quickly after reaching the 10-m mark?

....

....

....

....

3. **Interpret Data** Do your data seem reasonable for representing speeds and distances traveled by basketball players on a court? Explain why or why not.

....

....

....

....

4. **Provide Critique** Compare your procedure with the procedure of another group. What did that group do differently? What would you suggest to improve that group's procedure?

....

....

....

5. **Construct Arguments** Write a proposal to the school that explains the importance of making sure the basketball court has enough space around it. In your proposal, suggest a strategy for making the court safer. Cite data from your investigation as evidence to support your points.

....

....

....

....

....

Electricity and Magnetism

NGSS PERFORMANCE EXPECTATIONS

MS-PS2-3 Ask questions about data to determine the factors that affect the strength of electric and magnetic forces.

MS-PS2-5 Conduct an investigation and evaluate the experimental design to provide evidence that fields exist between objects exerting forces on each other even though the objects are not in contact.

MS-PS3-2 Develop a model to describe that when the arrangement of objects interacting at a distance changes, different amounts of potential energy are stored in the system.

HANDS-ON LAB

uConnect Make observations to determine the north and south poles of a magnet.

GO ONLINE
to access your
digital course

▶ VIDEO

👆 INTERACTIVITY

🧪 VIRTUAL LAB

☑ ASSESSMENT

📖 eTEXT

🧪 HANDS-ON LABS

How does pedaling generate electricity for the lights?

The Essential Question

What factors affect the strength of electric and magnetic forces?

When the rider pedals this bicycle, he generates electricity for the lights on the carousel. The process uses electromagnets. As the cyclist pedals faster, the lights become brighter. How do you think the action of pedaling produces light?

....

....

....

....

Quest KICKOFF

How can you lift an object without making contact?

STEM **Phenomenon** In Japan, South Korea, and China, you can hop on a train that uses electromagnets to levitate above a rail and travel at incredibly high speeds. The technology is the result of years of research and testing by electric and mechanical engineers. In this STEM Quest, you will explore how you can use electromagnetism to lift or raise objects without coming into contact with them. In digital activities, you will investigate electric and magnetic forces. By applying what you have learned, you will design, build, and test a device that can levitate objects.

👆 **INTERACTIVITY**

Light as a Feather?

MS-PS2-3 Ask questions about data to determine the factors that affect the strength of electric and magnetic forces.
MS-PS2-5 Conduct an investigation and evaluate the experimental design to provide evidence that fields exist between objects exerting forces on each other even though the objects are not in contact.
MS-PS3-2 Develop a model to describe that when the arrangement of objects interacting at a distance changes, different amounts of potential energy are stored in the system.

📺 NBC LEARN ▶ VIDEO

After watching the video, which examines some industrial applications of magnets and electromagnets, list two examples of objects that you use every day that rely on magnets or electromagnets.

Example 1

....

....

....

Example 2

....

....

....

Quest CHECK-IN

IN LESSON 1

STEM What kinds of forces are exerted by positive and negative charges? Think about how charged objects interact and apply what you have learned to your levitating device.

👆 **INTERACTIVITY**

Apply Electrical Forces

Quest CHECK-IN

IN LESSON 2

STEM How can you use magnets to build a levitation device? Develop possible design solutions by exploring magnetic forces.

HANDS-ON LAB

Tracking Levitation

Quest CHECK-IN

IN LESSON 3

STEM How can you control the strength of your device? Build an electromagnet and explore how you can incorporate the technology into your device.

HANDS-ON LAB

Building an Electromagnet

Magnetism is used to elevate this "maglev" train several centimeters above the tracks and also to propel it forward. The absence of friction between the train and the track allows the maglev train to achieve speeds up to 600 kilometers per hour!

Quest CHECK-IN

IN LESSON 4

STEM How can you refine your levitating device to improve your results? Redesign and retest your device using electromagnets.

HANDS-ON LAB

Electrifying Levitation

Quest FINDINGS

Complete the Quest!

Apply what you've learned by describing other scenarios in your daily life in which electromagnets could be used to make a task easier.

INTERACTIVITY

Reflect on Your Levitating Device

Electric Force

Guiding Questions

- What causes electric fields and electric forces?
- How is potential energy affected by positions of charges?
- How is static electricity different from current?

Connection

Literacy Integrate with Visuals

MS-PS2-5, MS-PS3-2

HANDS-ON LAB

ᴜInvestigate Use a device to detect electric charges.

Vocabulary

electron
electric force
electric field
electric current
conductor
static electricity

Academic Vocabulary

charge
neutral

Connect It !

✎ **Identify the parts of this picture that you think show the transfer of electric charges. Draw dots to indicate the paths of the moving electric charges from a cloud to the ground.**

Explain Why do you think lightning is so dangerous if it comes in contact with a person?

....

....

....

Electric Force, Fields, and Energy

Did you know that there are electric **charges**, forces, and fields inside your body? You might not see them or feel them, but they are in every atom, everywhere!

Atoms are made up of protons, neutrons, and electrons, as shown in **Figure 1**. Protons are positively charged particles, and **electrons** are negatively charged particles. Neutrons are **neutral**, meaning that they do not have a charge. Most objects are made of atoms in which the number of protons is equal to the number of electrons. As a result, the positive and negative charges cancel out and the atoms are neutral. However, electrons can move from one atom or object to another. If an object loses electrons, it is left with more protons than electrons. It has an overall positive charge. If an object gains electrons, it will have an overall negative charge.

If you have ever watched a lightning storm, as in **Figure 2**, you have seen a dramatic display of electric charges. The lightning bolts are made up of moving electrons.

☑ **READING CHECK** **Summarize Text** How can a neutral object become negatively charged?

....

....

Academic Vocabulary

Charge is a basic property of matter that creates a force and accounts for electric interactions. Some particles and atoms have no charge, so they are neutral. Is the atom in **Figure 1** neutral or charged?

....

Model of an Atom

Figure 1 Charged particles make up atoms.

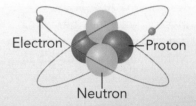

Electron — Proton

Neutron

Lightning Storm

Figure 2 Lightning bolts can travel from clouds to the ground. They can also travel within a cloud and between clouds. These streaks of light are the result of the movement of electric charges.

Electric Field Lines

Figure 3 Images A and B show the field lines around single charges. Image C shows the field lines around a positive charge and a negative charge next to each other. Where field lines are closer together, the electric field is stronger.

1. Use Models Is the electric field stronger within the white rectangle or within the blue rectangle in image C?

....

....

2. Draw Conclusions Is the electric field stronger close to the charges or further away from the charges?

....

....

☑ **READING CHECK** In which direction would a positive charge move if it were placed in between the positive and negative charges in image C?

....

....

Electric Force The force between charged particles or objects is called **electric force**. If a proton and an electron come close together, the opposition of their positive and negative forces creates an attraction that draws them together. On the other hand, if two electrons come close together, they repel each other because they both are negatively charged. The electric force causes them to move apart. In general, opposite charges attract, and like charges repel.

The strength of the electric force depends on the distance between the charges. For example, when a positively-charged particle or object is close another positively-charged particle, a strong force between them pushes them away from each other. As they move apart, the force between them becomes weaker. The strength of the electric force also depends on the amount of charge present. When more charge is involved, the electric force is stronger. For instance, three protons attract an electron more strongly than one proton alone.

Electric Fields Two charged particles will experience electric forces between them without even touching. How is this possible? An electric charge has an invisible **electric field** around it—a region around the charged particle or object where the electric force is exerted on other charged particles or objects. Electric fields can be represented by field lines, as in **Figure 3**. They point in the direction that the force would push a positive charge. Field lines around a positively charged object point away from the object. They indicate that the object would repel a positive charge. Field lines around a negatively charged object point toward the object. The negatively charged object would attract a positive charge. When multiple charges are in the same area, the field lines show a slightly more complicated combination of the two fields.

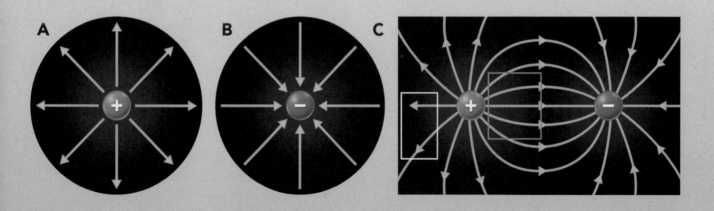

Charges and Potential Energy When forces are in action, you can be sure that energy is also involved. Suppose you have a system that consists of two opposite charges and their interaction. If you pull the opposite charges away from each other, the potential energy of the system increases. You can understand this by comparing it to gravitational potential energy. Gravity is an attractive force. When you lift an object higher above the ground, you apply a force and transfer energy to it. The object's gravitational potential energy increases. When you drop the object, the force of gravity pulls the object to the ground and its gravitational potential energy decreases. The force between opposite charges is also an attractive force. As you apply a force to move opposite charges away from each other, the electric potential energy of the system increases. When the electric force between opposite charges pulls them together naturally, the potential energy of the system decreases, as shown in **Figure 4**.

Potential energy changes in a different way between two like charges. Two like charges naturally repel each other. An outside force is not needed to move them apart. Therefore, as the electric force between two like charges pushes them away from each other, the potential energy of the system decreases.

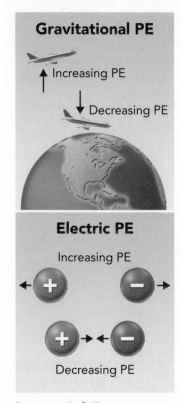

Potential Energy
Figure 4 Electric potential energy behaves a lot like gravitational potential energy.

Question It !

Students are conducting an experiment to provide evidence that electric fields exert forces on objects even when the objects are not in contact. They use pith balls hanging from strings. Pith balls are small balls that pick up charge easily. These pith balls have been charged by touching another charged object. The students drew this diagram to show the result of their experiment.

1. Cause and Effect When the two pith balls have opposite charges, they are naturally pulled together due to the attractive electric force between them. If you pull the two pith balls away from each other, what happens to the potential energy of the system? Explain.

   ....

   ....

   ....

2. Cite Evidence How do the results of this experiment provide evidence that electric fields exert forces on the pith balls, even when they are not in contact?

   ....

   ....

Electric Current and Circuits

Electric charges play a major role in daily life. Any time you use electricity, you are using energy from electric charges that are in motion. The charges flow through materials like water flows down a stream. The continuous flow of charge is known as **electric current**. Current is measured as a rate in units called amperes. The abbreviation for this unit is A. The number of amperes describes the amount of charge that passes by a given point each second.

Current flows through paths known as circuits. A circuit is a path that runs in a loop. A basic electric circuit contains a source of energy connected with wires to a device that runs on electricity. Current flows from the source of energy, through the wires, through the electric device, and back to the source.

Voltage Why do charges flow through a circuit? They move because of differences in potential energy. Current flows from a point of higher potential energy to a point of lower potential energy in the circuit. For instance, a battery, like the one shown in **Figure 5**, has one end where current has a higher potential energy per charge than it has at the other end of the battery. This difference in electric potential energy per charge is called voltage. The voltage acts like a force that causes current to flow. Voltage is measured in units of volts. The abbreviation for this unit is V.

Literacy Connection

Integrate with Visuals
✏ Draw dots and arrows to represent current flowing through the circuit.

Current in Circuits

Figure 5 The following circuit shows a battery connected to a light bulb. Based on potential energy, which direction should the current flow? Explain your answer.

....
....
....
....
....
....
....

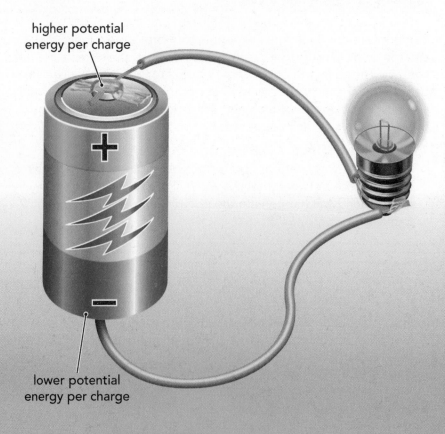

higher potential energy per charge

lower potential energy per charge

Energy in Circuits You can compare a charge in a circuit to an object in the gravitational field of Earth. When an object falls, the force of gravity pulls the object from a position of higher potential energy to a position of lower potential energy. You give that potential energy back when you lift the object up to its initial position. A battery gives energy back to charges as well. Inside the battery, the energy from chemical substances is converted to electric energy. That electric energy becomes the potential energy of the charges. They return to a position of higher potential energy, from which they flow through the circuit.

Current and Resistance What are the charges that flow through a circuit? They are electrons. Historically, the current is described as flowing in the direction in which positive charges would move. However, electrons are negatively charged. So the direction of current is opposite to the direction of electron flow.

Some materials have electrons that are tightly bound to their atoms. Their electrons are difficult to move. Those materials, called insulators, do not allow charge to flow. Therefore, they have a high resistance to electric current. On the other hand, some materials have electrons that are more loosely bound to their atoms. Those materials are **conductors**—they allow charge to flow more freely (**Figure 6**). Just as there are insulators and conductors of heat, there are insulators and conductors of charge. Insulators of charge are materials such as rubber, wood, and glass, while conductors include materials such as silver, copper, and gold.

✓ READING CHECK **Explain** Describe why current flows through a circuit, and explain why some materials allow charges to flow more easily than others.

....

....

....

....

Conductors and Insulators of Charge
Figure 6 Conductors and insulators of charge are all around you. Label each of these common items as a conductor or an insulator.

Integrate Information Which of the materials used to make these objects would you use in a circuit? Explain why.

....

....

....

....

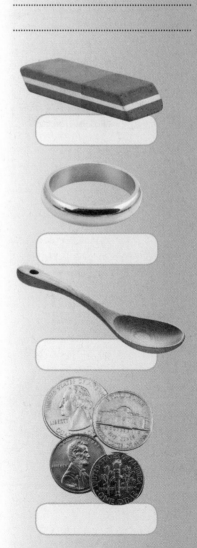

HANDS-ON LAB

Investigate Use a device to detect electric charges.

Charging by Induction

Figure 7 If your finger has a build-up of charge, it may induce a charge in a doorknob. Electrons in the doorknob move away from your finger to the opposite side of the doorknob.

Static Electricity

Recall that most objects are made of atoms in which the number of protons is equal to the number of electrons. As a result, these atoms are neutral. By the law of conservation of charge, charge cannot be created or destroyed, but it can be transferred. The transfer of charge happens by moving electrons from one object to another or from one part of an object to another. When charges build up on an object, they do not flow like current. Instead, they remain static, meaning they stay in place. This buildup of charge on an object is called **static electricity**.

Methods of Charging

Objects can become charged by four methods: conduction, friction, induction, and polarization. Charging by conduction is simply the movement of charge by direct contact between objects. The object that is more negatively charged transfers electrons to the other object. Charging by friction occurs when two objects rub against each other and electrons move from one object to the other. Objects become charged by induction without even touching. The electric field of one charged object repels the electrons of the other object. So the second object ends up with a buildup of charge on its opposite side, as in **Figure 7**. Polarization is similar except the electrons only move to the opposite side of their atoms rather than to the opposite side of the entire object. See if you can identify the methods of charging in **Figure 8**.

Interactions with Static Electricity

Figure 8 Label the method of charging in each image as conduction, friction, induction, or polarization.

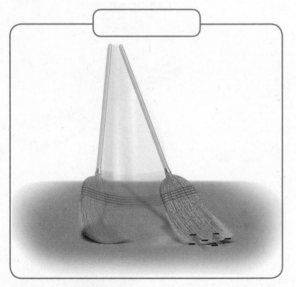

The broom becomes charged as it sweeps across the floor.

Bits of paper are attracted to the broom's negative charge. In the paper, electrons of the atoms move to the opposite side of each atom, away from the broom.

Balloon and Paper
Figure 9 🖊 The balloon attracts the paper because of static electricity. Draw the charges on the balloon and on the bits of paper. Then, describe what happens to potential energy as you pull the bits of paper off of the balloon.

....

....

....

....

....

Potential Energy and Static Electricity

If you rub a balloon, you might be surprised that it can pick up bits of paper. The balloon attracts the paper because of static electricity. Rubbing the balloon causes electrons to transfer to it. The charged balloon polarizes the bits of paper. Because the surface of the balloon is negatively charged and the surface of the paper is positively charged, they attract each other as in **Figure 9**. As the bits of paper move toward the balloon, the potential energy between the balloon and paper decreases. When you pull the bits of paper off of the balloon, you apply a force to them. The potential energy between the balloon and the paper increases the further you move them apart.

Static Discharge

Most objects that become charged eventually lose their charge to the air. Charge transfers to or from the air until the charged object is neutral. The process of discharging can sometimes cause a spark or shock when the electrons transfer. If you have ever reached to pet a cat and experienced a shock, it was the result of static discharge.

Lightning is also the result of static discharge. Water droplets in the clouds become charged due to all of the motion within the air during a storm. Electrons then move from areas of negative charge to areas of positive charge. The movement of charge produces the intense spark that we see as a lightning bolt.

☑ **READING CHECK** **Describe** What happens to charges during static discharge?

....

▶ **VIDEO**

Watch and learn how lightning works.

👆 **INTERACTIVITY**

Develop a model to show the potential energy of a system involving electric forces.

📓 **Reflect** Describe a time when you experienced a shock from static electricity. Explain what happened in terms of electric charges.

☑ LESSON 1 Check

MS-PS2-5, MS-PS3-2

1. **Describe** Why are conductors better than insulators for the flow of electric current?

....

....

....

....

2. **Explain** A proton is placed next to an negatively charged object. In which direction would the proton move? Explain why.

....

....

....

....

....

3. **Cause and Effect** If you move two objects with opposite charges apart, what happens to the potential energy between them? Explain your response.

....

....

....

....

....

4. **Develop Models** ✎ After Sandra combs her hair, she notices that her hair moves toward the comb. Draw a model of the comb and Sandra's hair. Show the charges on both the comb and the hair. Describe the types of charges that you think occurred to charge the comb and then to charge the hair.

....

....

....

....

....

....

....

Quest CHECK-IN

In this lesson, you learned about the interactions of electric charges through forces and fields. You also discovered how potential energy plays a role in the flow of current. Additionally, you explored how charges behave in static electricity.

Apply Scientific Reasoning How might electric fields become involved in your levitation device?

....

....

....

👆 INTERACTIVITY

Apply Electrical Forces

Go online to explore how the interaction between charged particles could be used to develop a design for a levitation device.

MS-PS2-5, MS-PS3-2

Bumblebees and Electric Flowers

Most people assume that bumblebees are attracted to certain flowers only because of their colors and scents. As it turns out, there's more to it!

Bumblebees also respond to flowers' electric fields! While the bee has a positive electric charge, the flower and its pollen usually have a negative charge. The opposite charges make the pollen cling to the bee's body.

Scientists believe that bumblebees can use the strength of a flower's electric field to tell how much pollen is there. If they can sense that the field has changed and another bee has already taken all the pollen, then they will move to another flower. Given the number of flowers a bee visits, this information would be really useful!

Bumblebees may use this electric sense for many things, such as recognizing landmarks or identifying which bees have been in a garden before them. Although the bumblebee population is declining, perhaps scientists can find a way to use the bees' electric sense to help save them.

MY DISCOVERY

With a classmate, come up with some questions you have about the relationship between bees and flowers. How might this information be helpful in restoring the bumblebee population? What sources might you investigate to find answers?

② Magnetic Force

Guiding Questions

- How can you change the magnetic force and potential energy between objects?
- How can you detect and describe a magnetic field?

Connection

Literacy Verify

MS-PS2-5, MS-PS3-2

HANDS-ON LAB

uInvestigate Discover how you can use a magnet to tell the difference between real and fake coins.

Vocabulary

magnet
magnetism
magnetic force
magnetic pole
magnetic field

Academic Vocabulary

interaction

Connect It !

✏️ **Magnetic field lines are drawings that represent the invisible force around a magnet. Trace one of the magnetic field lines on this page.**

Translate Information How can you describe the shape of Earth's magnetic field?

....

Use Models What does the model show about Earth's magnetic field?

....

....

Identify Limitations What is a limitation of this two-dimensional model?

....

Magnetic Force and Energy

You may use magnets to display notes or pictures on the door of the refrigerator. A **magnet** attracts iron and materials that contain iron. Magnets can be any size, from the ones you use in the kitchen to the entire Earth and beyond. People can use magnetic compasses in navigation because the whole planet acts as a magnet (**Figure 1**).

Magnets attract iron and some other materials—usually metals. They attract or repel other magnets. This attraction or repulsion is called **magnetism**. The **interaction** between a magnet and a substance containing iron is always an attraction. Magnets themselves can either attract or repel one another, depending on how they are placed.

Magnetism can be a permanent or temporary property of a material. Some materials, containing iron or certain other metals, can become permanent magnets after interacting with other magnets. On the other hand, temporary magnetism can occur in different ways. An iron or steel object that is touching a magnet can become a magnet itself as long as the contact exists. For example, you can make a chain of paper clips that hangs from a permanent magnet. Another type of temporary magnet is created when an electric current flows through a conductor. This kind of magnet exists as long as the current is flowing.

Academic Vocabulary

The term *interaction* comes from words meaning *action* and *between* two things. Describe an interaction that you had today.

....

....

....

Magnetic Force

Figure 1 Lines and arrows show the direction of the magnetic field around Earth.

INTERACTIVITY

Examine magnetic objects and their fields.

Magnetic Force

Magnetism is caused by a force that can act at a distance. This **magnetic force** is a push or pull that occurs when a magnet interacts with another object. Some large magnets can attract objects from many meters away and are powerful enough to lift a car or truck.

How do you know if the magnetic force between two objects will be a push or a pull? A magnet always exerts a pull on a magnetic object that is not itself a magnet. If you place the ends of the horseshoe magnet in **Figure 2** near a pile of paper clips, the paper clips always move toward the magnet. They never move away. Every magnet has two ends, called **magnetic poles**, where the magnetic force is strongest. One pole is known as the north pole and the other is known as the south pole.

The arrangement of magnets determines which type of force exists between them. If you bring two magnets together so that *like* poles—either both north or both south—are near one another, the magnets repel. If you bring the magnets together so that opposite poles are close to one another, the magnets attract. **Figure 2** shows two ways in which bar magnets can interact.

Push or Pull

Figure 2 ✎ Magnets can either push or pull. Draw arrows on the paperclips and on the bar magnets to show the direction of the magnetic force.

Magnets and Potential Energy

Recall the ways in which the potential energy of a system of electrical charges can change. As you apply a force to move opposite charges away from each other, the electric potential energy of the system increases. The same is true of magnets. Opposite poles naturally attract each other, so you must put energy into the system to pull them apart. As you apply a force to separate the two opposite poles, the potential energy of the system increases. When the magnetic force between opposite poles pulls them together the potential energy of the system decreases. On the other hand, like poles repel each other. To push them together, you have to transfer energy to the system. This increases the potential energy of the system. Use the **Figure 3** activity to summarize these changes in potential energy.

HANDS-ON LAB

Investigate Discover how you can use a magnet to tell the difference between real and fake coins.

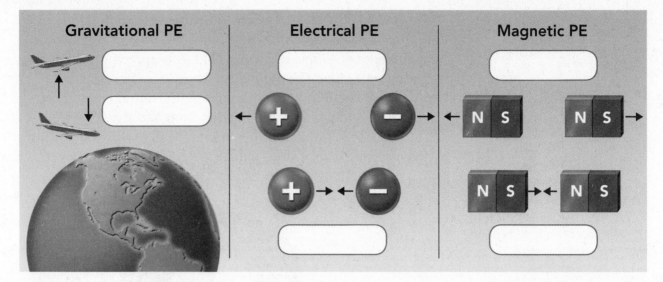

Gravitational PE	Electrical PE	Magnetic PE

Magnetic Fields

The magnetic force is strongest at a magnet's poles. That is why the paper clips tend to stick to the horseshoe magnet at its ends. There is an area of magnetic force that surrounds a magnet. This area of force is the **magnetic field** of the magnet. This field is the source of magnetic energy. It allows magnets to attract objects at a distance. The magnetic field extends from one pole to the other pole of the magnet. You cannot see a magnetic field, but if you place tiny pieces of iron near a magnet, they will arrange themselves along the magnetic field. Their arrangement looks a lot like lines, so illustrations of magnetic fields are drawn with lines, as shown in **Figure 4**.

Objects containing iron, such as steel paper clips, experience a force when they are in a magnetic field. These objects line up with the field around them. Particles inside the objects can also line up with the field. When the particles in an object line up with the field, the object becomes a temporary magnet.

Potential Energy
Figure 3 The gravitational force between the plane and Earth is an attractive force. The forces between opposite charges and opposite magnetic poles are also attractive. Label the locations of increasing and decreasing potential energy in the images.

Visualizing Magnetic Fields
Figure 4 The magnetic field around a bar magnet causes iron filings to form the arrangement shown. This arrangement can also be represented by magnetic field lines. The field is strongest where the lines are closest together.

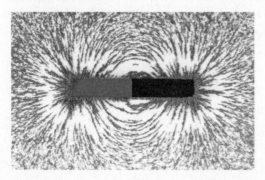
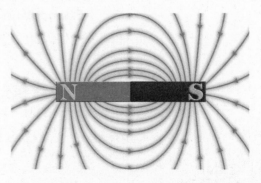

Single Magnetic Field The lines in **Figure 4** and **Figure 5** show a single magnetic field—a field that is produced by one magnet. Single magnetic field lines spread out from one pole, curve around the magnet to the other pole, and make complete loops. Arrows on the lines point from the north pole to the south pole to indicate the direction of the field. When the lines are close together, the magnetic field is stronger than it is where the lines are far apart. Magnetic field lines never cross one another.

Magnetic Field Lines

Figure 5 These lines show the shape of the field around the magnetic poles of a horseshoe magnet.

1. Patterns ✏ Add labels to the illustration to show where the magnetic field is strongest and where it is weakest.

2. Use Models Could you pick up a nail using the curved part of the horseshoe magnet farthest from the poles? Explain your answer.

....

....

....

....

....

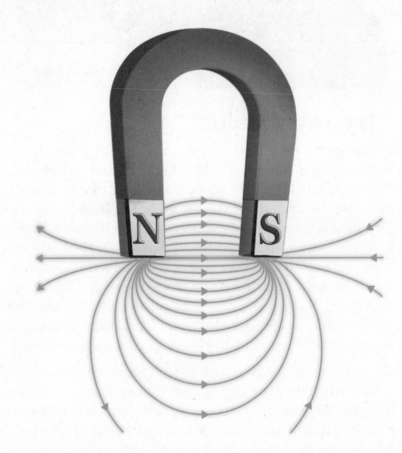

Combined Magnetic Field The magnetic fields of two magnets placed near each other will interact with one another. When two like poles are close together, the poles and the magnetic fields around them repel one another. When two opposite poles are close together, the fields combine to form a strong magnetic field between the two magnets, as shown in **Figure 6**. As in a single magnetic field, the lines never cross one another.

☑ **READING CHECK Identify** What does the distance between magnetic field lines indicate?

....

....

Combined Magnetic Field Lines

Figure 6 The image on the left shows the combined magnetic field when opposite poles of bar magnets face each other.

Develop Models What would the magnetic field look like if like poles faced each other?

✎ Draw a model of the magnetic field lines in the image on the right.

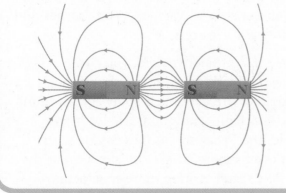

Earth's Magnetic Field

Earth's Magnetic Field Earth itself acts as a very large magnet. Materials in the core of the planet generate a magnetic field that surrounds the planet. This magnetic field is very similar to the field that surrounds a bar magnet. The magnetic poles of Earth are located near the geographic poles. These are the points where the magnetic field is strongest. The magnetic field lines pass out of the core and through the rocky mantle. They also loop through the space surrounding Earth. The magnetic field is three-dimensional and it is shaped like a donut, as shown in **Figure 7**.

People have used this magnetic field for many centuries for navigation. A compass, shown in **Figure 7**, is a magnetized needle that can turn easily. The needle interacts with Earth's magnetic field. One end is attracted to the north magnetic pole and the other end to the south magnetic pole. People can use a compass to determine the direction in which they are traveling.

 VIDEO

See how magnetic fields interact.

Compass
Figure 7 Sailors and hikers use a compass to determine direction. The needle always points toward the geographic north pole. This is the pole that we call the North Pole, but because it is actually a south magnetic pole, the magnetic field lines point toward it.

INTERACTIVITY

Explore magnetic forces and potential energy using models.

Literacy Connection

Verify Use a reliable Internet source to verify that Earth's magnetic field is caused by substances inside the planet. Which source did you use? How do you know that it's reliable?

....

....

....

....

Aurora Borealis

Figure 8 Auroras form when Earth's magnetic field pushes charged particles toward the poles. The high-energy particles interact with molecules in the atmosphere.

Protecting Life on Earth There is a constant stream of particles that flows from the sun toward Earth. This stream is known as the solar wind. These particles have electric charges and they have a lot of energy as they move very rapidly through space. If they were to reach the surface of Earth, the particles in the stream could harm living things. Fortunately, Earth's magnetic field protects us. Electrically charged particles interact with magnetic forces. Earth's magnetic field changes the motion of the charged particles. They flow toward the north and south poles and then past Earth into space. You will learn more about the relationship between electric charges and magnetic fields in the following lessons.

Although you cannot see this protective field, you can sometimes see evidence of it working. Auroras, sometimes called the "Northern Lights," are glowing displays in the night sky. As these energetic electrically charged particles travel along the magnetic field lines, they sometimes collide with gas atoms in the upper atmosphere. These collisions cause the atoms to give off light. The result is often more spectacular than a fireworks show (**Figure 8**).

✓ READING CHECK **Use Evidence** Describe how the Aurora Borealis is evidence that the Earth has a magnetic field.

....

....

....

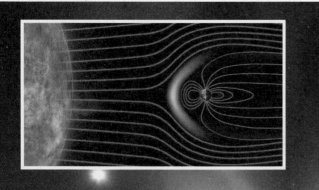

✅ LESSON 2 Check

1. **Identify** How can you identify the magnetic north pole of an unlabeled magnet by using a labeled magnet?

....

....

....

....

2. **Patterns** How would increasing the magnetic force of a magnet change the pattern of magnetic field lines between its poles?

....

....

3. **Apply Concepts** Explain how potential energy changes when you pull a magnet off a refrigerator door.

....

....

....

....

4. **Construct an Explanation** Why is the electrical charge on particles in the solar wind an important element of the protection that Earth's magnetic field provides?

....

....

....

5. **Develop Models** ✏️ Draw the magnetic field lines around a nail which has its head as its north pole and its point as its south pole.

In this lesson, you discovered magnetic fields and how to draw the lines that represent them. You also learned how potential energy changes when a magnet is present.

Describe how you could orient two magnets so that they repel each other. How might this apply to your levitation device?

....

....

....

....

HANDS-ON LAB

Tracking Levitation

Go online to download the lab worksheet. You will consider how a stable train and section of track can be built using permanent magnets.

Electromagnetic Force

Guiding Questions

- How does electricity relate to magnetism?
- How can you describe the magnetic field produced by a current?
- What are the properties of solenoids and electromagnets?

Connections

Literacy Cite Textual Evidence

Math Draw Comparative Inferences

MS-PS2-3

HANDS-ON LAB

ᴜInvestigate Explore the relationship between electricity and magnetism.

Vocabulary

electromagnetism
solenoid
electromagnet

Academic Vocabulary

produce

Connect It !

✏ **Circle the magnet in the photo.**

Explain Phenomena How do you know that the object picking up the metal beams is a magnet?

....

....

Support Your Explanation What material do you think makes up this magnet?

....

Electromagnetic Principles

Have a look at **Figure 1**. How is this crane's magnet strong enough to lift these heavy metal beams? The answer may surprise you. The magnetic field of this crane is actually generated by an electric current! The relationship between electricity and magnetism is called **electromagnetism**.

Electromagnetism was first discovered by a scientist named Hans Christian Ørsted. During a class he was teaching, he brought a compass near a wire that had an electric current running through it. He noticed that the compass needle changed direction when it was near the wire. He placed several different compasses near a wire and found out that the compass needles changed direction when a current passed through the wire. The compass needles did not change direction when no current flowed. Ørsted concluded that an electric current produces a magnetic field, so electricity and magnetism are related.

Literacy Connection

Cite Textual Evidence What evidence did Ørsted use to conclude that an electric current produces a magnetic field?

....

....

....

....

....

Write About It In your science notebook, describe a time that you drew a new conclusion from your observations.

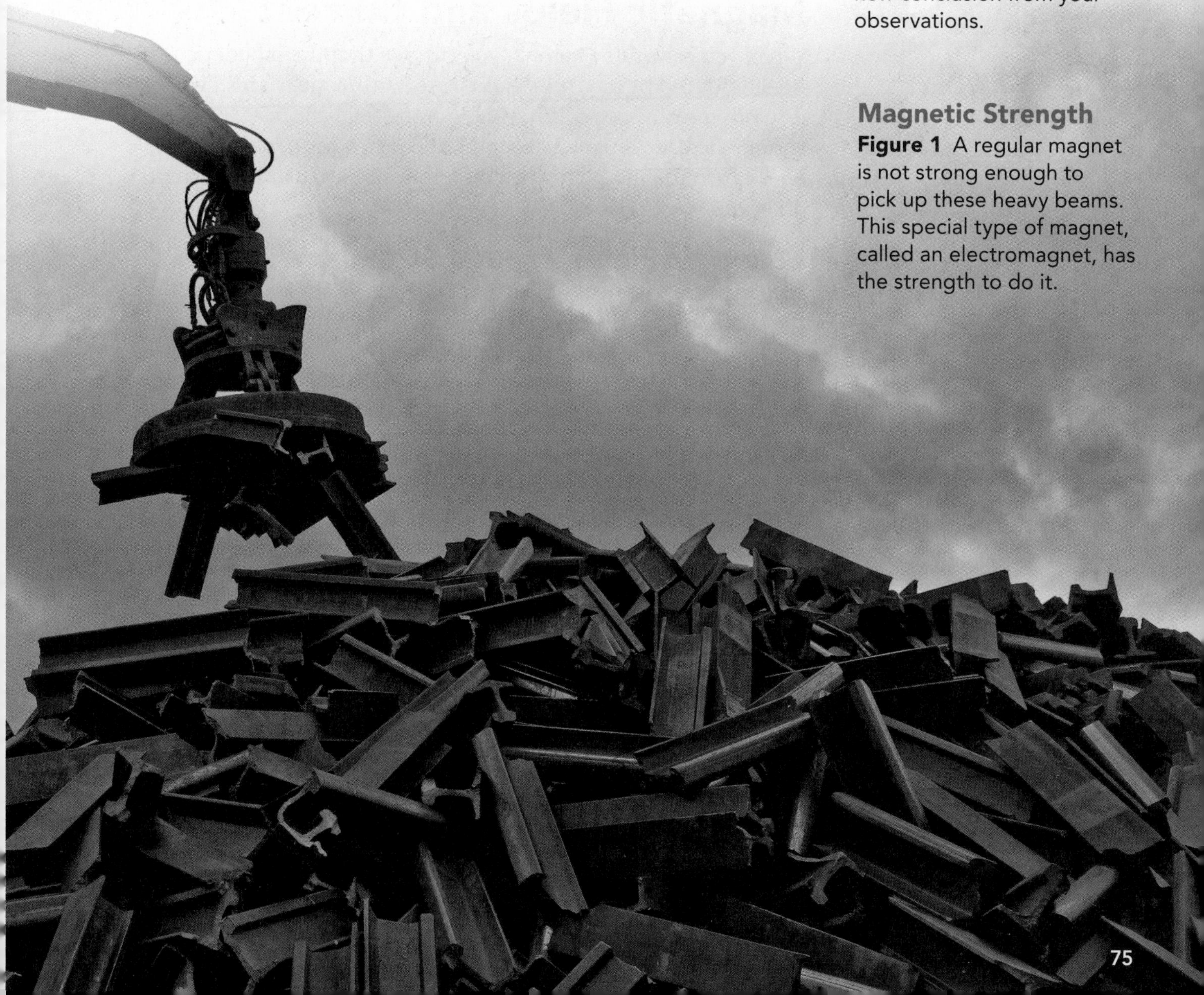

Magnetic Strength

Figure 1 A regular magnet is not strong enough to pick up these heavy beams. This special type of magnet, called an electromagnet, has the strength to do it.

Magnetism from Electricity

Figure 2 🖊 This figure shows how the direction of a current in a straight wire affects the magnetic field that forms. In the image on the left, the current flows upward. Draw your predicted magnetic field lines in the image on the right, in which the current flows downward.

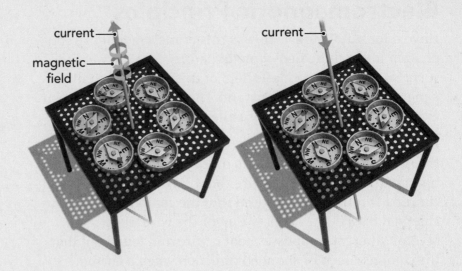

current —
magnetic field

current —

Current

Magnetic field

The Right-Hand Rule

Figure 3 Imagine that you are holding the wire in your right hand with your thumb pointing in the direction the current flows. The direction of the magnetic field is the same as the direction that your fingers curl.

Magnetic Fields and Current

When you examine **Figure 2**, you can see that the magnetic field produced by a current has a certain direction. This field also has a certain strength. How can the field change? It can change in direction and strength, and it can be turned off or on. To turn the magnetic field off or on, simply turn the current off or on.

Magnetic Fields Around Straight Wires
In a straight wire, the field's direction depends on the direction of the current. How do you determine the direction of a magnetic field based on the direction of current through a straight wire? You can use what is known as the right-hand rule, as shown in **Figure 3**.

To change the strength of a magnetic field around a current-carrying straight wire, change the amount of current running through the wire. If current is increased, the magnetic field becomes stronger. If the current is decreased, the strength of the magnetic field decreases.

✅ **READING CHECK** **Determine Central Ideas** How do electric currents relate to magnetic fields?

....

....

Magnetic Fields Around Wire Loops

Suppose you have a loop of wire rather than a straight wire. The magnetic field formed around the loop of wire is in many ways like the field formed when a current flows through a straight wire. The direction of the field depends on the direction of the current and can be determined by using the right-hand rule. The field can be turned off or on by turning the current off or on. The strength of the field depends on the strength of the current.

There is one main difference, however, when a current flows through a loop of wire. Look at **Figure 4**, which shows a current flowing through a loop of wire and the magnetic field it produces. Shaping a wire into a loop can increase the strength of the magnetic field within the loop.

☑ READING CHECK **Cause and Effect** You have a straight wire with a current running through it. What effect will looping the wire have on the magnetic field?

....

INTERACTIVITY

Predict the direction of magnetic field lines around a current-carrying wire.

Model It!

Magnetic Field Strength

Figure 4 The overhead view of a magnetic field formed by a current flowing through a single wire is shown. The magnetic field lines are closest together in the center of the loop, where the magnetic field is stronger. The number of loops in a wire can control the strength of a magnetic field.

1. **Develop Models** ✎ Draw the magnetic field lines around the two stacked loops of wire.

2. **Use Models** Is the strength of the magnetic field inside the loop greater or less than the strength when there was just one loop of wire? Justify your answer.

....

....

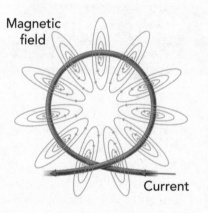

Magnetic field

Current

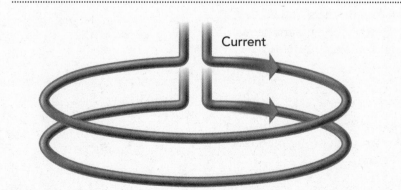

Current

INTERACTIVITY

Design and build a virtual electromagnet that can pick up objects.

Solenoids and Electromagnets

There are many practical uses of coiling a current-carrying wire to make a strong magnetic field. Two devices that strengthen a magnetic field by running a current through coiled wire are solenoids and electromagnets. A **solenoid** is a coil of wire with a current running through it, as shown in **Figure 5**. It is similar to stacked loops of wire. In a solenoid, the magnetic field is strengthened in the center of the coil when a current runs through the coil. One end of a solenoid acts like the north pole of a magnet, and the other end acts like the south pole.

Solenoids

Figure 5 The image shows the magnetic field lines around a solenoid.

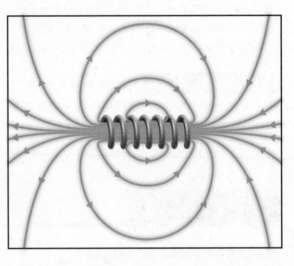

Math Toolbox

Solenoids and Magnetic Fields

A scientist conducted an experiment to investigate how different factors affect the strength of a magnetic field in the center of a solenoid. The solenoid was made of iron wire. In the experiment, the scientist changed the current passing through the wire and the number of coils per unit length of the solenoid. The results of the experiment are shown in the table. Tesla is the SI unit for the strength of a magnetic field.

Number of Coils per meter	Current (amps)	Magnetic Field Strength (Tesla)
100	1	20,000
200	1	40,000
100	2	40,000
200	2	80,000

1. **Draw Comparative Inferences** From the data shown, how does the current affect the strength of the magnetic field, if the number of coils per meter remains the same?

....

....

2. **Reason Quantitatively** From the data shown, how does the number of coils per meter affect the strength of the magnetic field, if current is constant?

....

....

Field Strength and Solenoids

You can increase the strength of the magnetic field inside a solenoid by increasing the number of coils or loops of wire. Winding the coils closer together also produces a stronger magnetic field. As in a straight wire, increasing the current through the solenoid wire will also increase the magnetic field.

INTERACTIVITY

Apply your knowledge of electromagnets and factors that affect electromagnetic force.

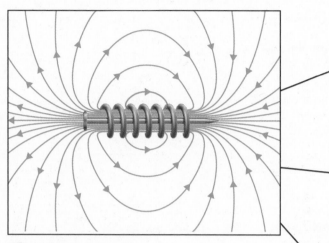

Electromagnets

Figure 6 A solenoid with a nail in the core is a simple electromagnet. More advanced electromagnets have many practical uses.

Some doors are locked with electromagnets and can only be unlocked electronically.

Electromagnets are used both to lift this train off the track and to propel it forward.

Electromagnets

What else can you do to a solenoid to make the magnetic field even stronger? You add a ferromagnetic material to it. A ferromagnetic material is a substance that becomes a magnet when exposed to a magnetic field. The elements iron, nickel and cobalt are ferromagnetic. As shown in **Figure 6**, a solenoid with a ferromagnetic core is called an **electromagnet**. When a ferromagnetic material is placed within a solenoid, both the current and the magnetized material **produce** a magnetic field. This combination produces a magnetic field that is stronger than that produced by the solenoid alone. As in a solenoid, the magnetic field of an electromagnet increases when the number of coils , the closeness of the coils, or the current increases.

Think back to the electromagnet you saw in **Figure 1**. How might you get the electromagnet to drop the metal beams? Just as with other magnetic fields caused by currents, you turn off the current. The magnetic field no longer exists, and the beams drop. Some other uses for electromagnets are shown in **Figure 6**.

An electromagnet helps to produce the vibrations in these earphones. These vibrations carry sound to your ears.

Academic Vocabulary

The term *produce* has several meanings. What does it mean in the text on this page?

....

....

✓ READING CHECK **Summarize** What is the structural difference between a solenoid and an electromagnet?

MS-PS2-3

1. Explain What did Ørsted discover about electricity and magnetism?

....

....

2. Cause and Effect Suppose that an electric current flows in a straight wire. The current changes so that it flows in the opposite direction. What changes occur in the magnetic field, and what stays the same?

....

....

....

3. Develop Models 🖉 A straight wire has a current running through it. Draw the current-carrying wire and the magnetic field that it produces.

4. Compare and Contrast Compare and contrast a solenoid and an electromagnet. What do they have in common? How are they different?

....

....

....

....

....

....

....

....

....

5. Apply Concepts An MRI machine uses an electromagnet to obtain scans of the human body. It uses these scans to generate images. What advantage is there in using an electromagnet instead of a solenoid in an MRI machine?

....

....

....

....

Quest CHECK-IN

In this lesson, you learned about electromagnetism and how electric currents generate magnetic fields. You also discovered how solenoids and electromagnets increase the strength of the magnetic fields.

Use Information How might you apply the principles of electromagnetism when building your levitating device?

....

....

....

....

HANDS-ON LAB

Building an Electromagnet

Go online to download the lab worksheet. Build an electromagnetic and determine how to control the strength of the electromagnetic force.

MS-PS2-3

ELECTROMAGNETISM
In Action

▶ VIDEO

Explore examples of electromagnetism.

How can you combine electric and magnetic forces to play a game or accomplish a task? You engineer it!

▶ **The Challenge:** To engineer devices that rely on elecromagnetic force.

Phenomenon People have known for centuries that electricity sparks and that magnets attract. The magnetic compass, for example, has been around since at least the 13th century, and possibly a great deal longer. But it was only in modern times that scientists and engineers began to understand that electricity and magnetism could affect each other.

Electromagnets differ from ordinary magnets because they only attract or repel when an electric current runs through them. An engineer can control an electromagnet, making it useful in industrial applications.

MRI and pinball machines are just two examples of the many devices that use electromagnets!

Electromagnetics govern a wide variety of devices and games, from a simple pinball machine to the Large Hadron Collider, an underground experimental facility that physicists are using to study particles. Hospitals use electromagnetics in procedures such as Magnetic Resonance Imaging (MRI). The music industry has found many uses for electromagnets—in speakers, headphones, complex percussion instruments, and recording equipment. Transportation is another field that makes extensive use of electromagnetic technology. The high-speed maglev trains use electromagnetic force to hover above the train tracks and whisk passengers to their destinations at speeds up to 600 kilometers per hour.

DESIGN CHALLENGE What can you design and build with an electromagnet? Go to the Engineering Design Notebook to find out!

Electric and Magnetic Interactions

Guiding Questions

- How do magnetic fields affect moving charges?
- How can current be produced in a conductor?
- How do generators and transformers work?

Connections

Literacy Draw Evidence

Math Understand Ratio Concepts

MS-PS2-3

HANDS-ON LAB

иInvestigate Discover the factors that affect the strength of electric and magnetic forces in a motor.

Vocabulary

galvanometer
electric motor
electromagnetic
  induction
generator
transformer

Academic Vocabulary

source

Connect It!

🖊 **Circle the part of the image that shows that electrical energy has been transformed into mechanical energy.**

Construct Explanations Explain how you think the fan works.

....

....

....

Identify List two other examples in which electrical energy transforms into mechanical energy.

....

....

Magnetic Force on Moving Charges

If a charged particle is at rest in a magnetic field, it is not affected by the field. But if the charged particle moves, it experiences a magnetic force. Why does this happen?

Recall that electric current is charged particles in motion. Suppose you have a wire with a current flowing through it, and you place it at rest in a magnetic field between two magnets. In this situation, there are two magnetic fields at play. The first field is caused by the magnets. The second field is caused by the current flowing through the wire. The magnetic field of the magnets interacts with the magnetic field around the wire. This interaction results in a force on the wire and causes the wire to move in the same direction as the force. The resulting force on the wire is perpendicular to the magnetic field, as given by another right-hand rule. This right-hand rule explains the direction a current-carrying wire moves in a magnetic field, as shown in **Figure 1**.

How does the fan in **Figure 2** work? Inside the fan is an electric motor. The motor uses interactions between magnetic fields around loops of wire and magnetic fields between magnets. To understand how the motor works, take a look at how a current-carrying loop of wire is affected by a magnetic field.

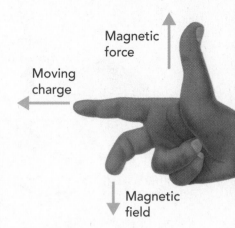

Magnetic force

Moving charge

Magnetic field

Right-Hand Rule #2
Figure 1 Point your index finger in the direction of the current, and bend your middle finger so that it points in the direction of the magnetic field. Your thumb points in the direction of the magnetic force on the moving charges.

Transforming into Mechanical Energy
Figure 2 The blades of this fan start moving when current flows into the fan.

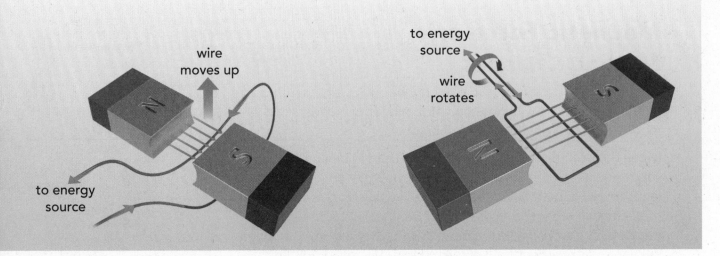

wire moves up

to energy source

to energy source

wire rotates

Current in a Magnetic Field

Figure 3 A straight wire moves in one direction in a magnetic field. A loop of wire rotates.

Loop of Current in a Magnetic Field If a straight wire with a current through it moves in the direction of the force on it, what happens when that wire forms a loop? Compare the two situations in **Figure 3**. When a single wire of current is placed in a magnetic field, it moves in one direction. But when a loop of current is placed in that same field, it rotates. In the loop, the current flows in one direction on one side of the loop. On the other side of the loop, the current flows in the opposite direction. As a result, the magnetic force on one side of the loop points up, and on the other side, the force points down. Because of the directions of these forces, the loop does not rotate in a complete circle. It rotates only half a turn, moving from horizontal to vertical.

Galvanometers This type of rotation is the basis of a **galvanometer**, which is a device that measures small currents. Showing how much current is flowing has many uses, such as in fuel gauges or even lie detectors. **Figure 4** shows a galvanometer. In this device, an electromagnet is suspended between two permanent magnets and is attached to the needle of the galvanometer. Recall that one way the strength of an electromagnet is determined is by the amount of current supplied to it. In a galvanometer, the current supplied to the electromagnet is the current that is being measured. If the current is extremely small, the force created is also small, and the needle rotates only a small amount. For a larger current, the force is greater, and the needle moves more.

INTERACTIVITY

Design and build a virtual motor for a model airplane.

Galvanometer

Figure 4 An electromagnet in the galvanometer turns the pointer to indicate the amount of current present. Why does an electromagnet act like a loop of wire in a magnetic field?

....

....

....

Electric Motors Recall the fan you saw in **Figure 1**, which contains a motor. An **electric motor** is a device that uses an electric current to turn an axle. In doing that, it transforms electrical energy into mechanical energy.

Examine **Figure 5** to learn the parts that make up an electric motor and how they work together to produce mechanical energy. Recall that a simple loop of wire in a magnetic field can only rotate half a turn because the current flows in only one direction. However, the brushes and the commutator enable the current that flows through the armature to change direction. Each time the commutator moves to a different brush, the current flows in the opposite direction. Thus, the side of the armature that just moved up will now move down, and the armature rotates continuously in one direction. Just picture the armature of a motor attached to an axle to which the blades of a fan are connected. Start the current, and feel the breeze!

✓ **READING CHECK** **Determine Differences** What is the only part of a motor through which a current does not flow?

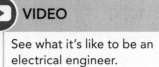

VIDEO

See what it's like to be an electrical engineer.

HANDS-ON LAB

Investigate Discover the factors that affect the strength of electric and magnetic forces in a motor.

How a Motor Works

Figure 5 🖉 A motor is made of several basic parts, each of which is described below. Study the information about each part. Then, write the number of each description in the appropriate circle on the image.

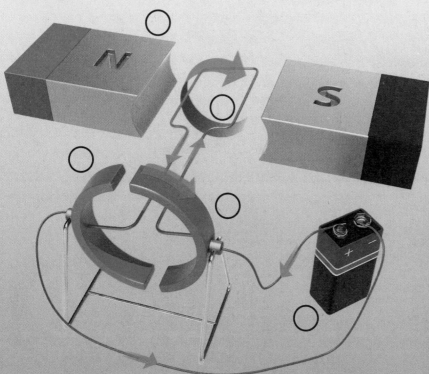

1. **Permanent magnets** produce a magnetic field. This causes the armature to turn.

2. The **commutator** consists of two semicircular pieces of metal. It conducts current from the brushes to the armature.

3. **Brushes,** which do not move, conduct current to the rest of the commutator.

4. The **armature** is a loop of wire that current flows through.

5. The **battery** is the energy source that supplies the current to the brushes.

VIDEO

Watch electromagnetic induction in action.

Literacy Connection

Draw Evidence Underline the sentence in the text which identifies the transformation of energy that occurs during electromagnetic induction.

Electromagnetic Induction

You've seen how a current flowing through a wire produces a magnetic field, and how electrical energy can be transformed into mechanical energy. In fact, the opposite is also possible. A magnetic field can be used to produce a current. If a conductor is moving through a magnetic field, a current is generated in the conductor. **Electromagnetic induction** is the process of generating an electric current from the motion of a conductor through a magnetic field. In this case, mechanical energy is transformed into electrical energy. The resulting current is called an induced current.

Induced Current and Moving Conductors

By experimentation, scientists discovered that when a conductor is moved in a magnetic field, a current flows through the conductor. Current can be induced if the conductor is a straight wire, as shown in **Figure 6**. The same principle applies if the conductor is a coil of wire. Induced current is present any time that a conductor moves through a magnetic field.

Induction from a Moving Wire

Figure 6 When a conductor (such as a metal wire) moves through a magnetic field, current will be induced in the conductor.

Interpret Diagrams Examine the image. Then, use the term *clockwise* or *counterclockwise* to complete each sentence correctly.

When the conductor moves upward through the magnetic field, the induced current flows _____.
When the conductor moves downward, the induced current is _____.

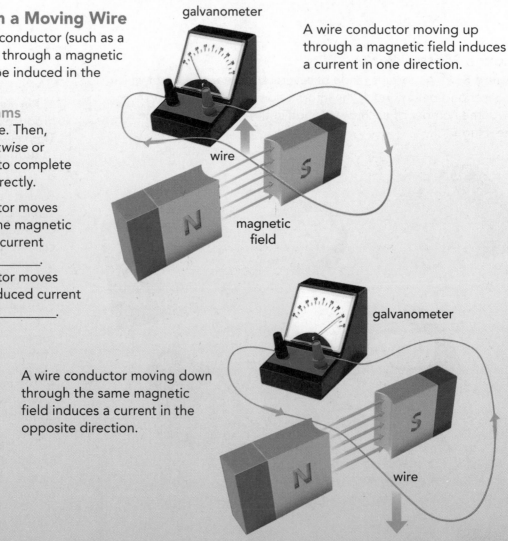

galvanometer

A wire conductor moving up through a magnetic field induces a current in one direction.

wire

magnetic field

A wire conductor moving down through the same magnetic field induces a current in the opposite direction.

galvanometer

wire

Induced Current and Moving Magnets

Induced Current and Moving Magnets As you have read, an electric current is induced when a conductor moves through a magnetic field. A current also is induced when a magnet moves through a loop of conductive wire. Examine **Figure 7**, which shows what happens when a magnet moves through a loop of wire.

In summary, electric current is induced in a conductor whenever the magnetic field around the conductor is changing. When a conductor is in a magnetic field, a current is induced in the conductor whenever either the conductor or the magnetic field is moving.

☑ READING CHECK **Integrate with Visuals** Based on Figure 6 and Figure 7, what are the two ways that a magnetic field can change, relative to a conductor?

....

....

....

👆 **INTERACTIVITY**

Predict the direction of a current through a wire near a moving magnet.

Induction from a Moving Magnet

Figure 7 Current will be induced in a conductor in a magnetic field when the magnetic field moves in relation to the conductor.

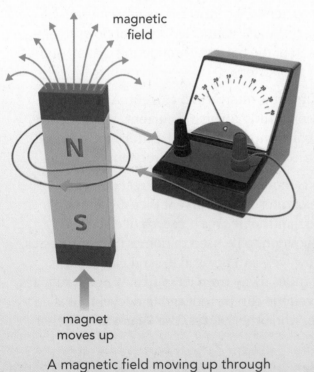

magnetic field

N

S

magnet moves up

A magnetic field moving up through a wire conductor induces a current in one direction.

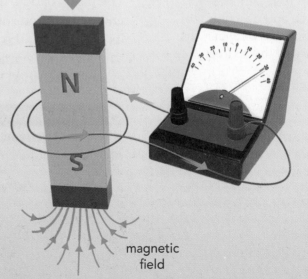

magnet moves down

A magnetic field moving down through a wire conductor induces a current in the opposite direction.

N

S

magnetic field

Types of Current

Figure 8 It is not uncommon for one object to require both direct and alternating currents to operate.

Ask Questions An electric car is one item that requires both AC and DC. Write a question about the use of AC and DC in the car.

....

....

....

Alternating and Direct Current

You have probably noticed that not all electrical currents are alike. The type of current that comes from a battery is direct current. Direct current, or DC, has charges that flow in only one direction. Objects that run on batteries use direct current. In these objects, opposite ends of the battery are connected to opposite ends of the circuit. When everything is connected, current flows in one direction from one end of the battery, through the circuit, and into the other end of the battery.

The other type of current is alternating current. Alternating current, or AC, is a constantly reversing current. When a wire in a magnetic field constantly changes direction, the induced current it produces also keeps changing direction.

Alternating current is more common than direct current because the voltage of alternating current is easily changed. For example, the current that leaves a **source** of electrical power has voltage too high to be used in homes and businesses. The high voltage, however, can be used to send electrical energy hundreds of miles away from its source. When it reaches its destination, the voltage can be reduced to a level that is safe for use in homes and other places. Use **Figure 8** to further examine AC and DC.

Academic Vocabulary

Think of one thing you have eaten today. Identify its source and describe the relationship between the food and the source.

....

....

....

✓ READING CHECK **Determine Central Ideas** What is the main difference between AC and DC?

....

....

Generators and Transformers

Two common and important devices that use induced current are generators and transformers. Generators and transformers are alike in that an electrical current leaves both of them. They differ in that generators produce electricity, and transformers change the voltage to make the electricity useful.

How Generators Work An electric generator transforms mechanical energy into an electric current. The movement of a conductor within a magnetic field produces a current. The essential parts of a generator are the armature, slip rings, magnets, brushes, and a crank. **Figure 9** shows what these parts are and how they all work together to produce an alternating electric current. The basic operation of a small home generator is the same as that of a large generator that provides current to many homes and businesses.

Although a generator contains some of the same parts as an electric motor, the two devices work in reverse. In an electric motor, an existing current produces a magnetic field, and electrical energy is transformed into mechanical energy. In a generator, the motion of a coil of wire through a magnetic field produces a current and mechanical energy is transformed into electrical energy.

INTERACTIVITY

Construct a virtual generator that can charge a cell phone.

INTERACTIVITY

Explore how electricity and magnetism affect the motion of various materials.

How a Generator Works

Figure 9 A generator works when its component parts operate in the correct order. Number the part names in the correct order to show the operation of a generator from the magnets to the moment when the current is produced. Then, circle the names of the parts of the generator that you would also find in an electric motor.

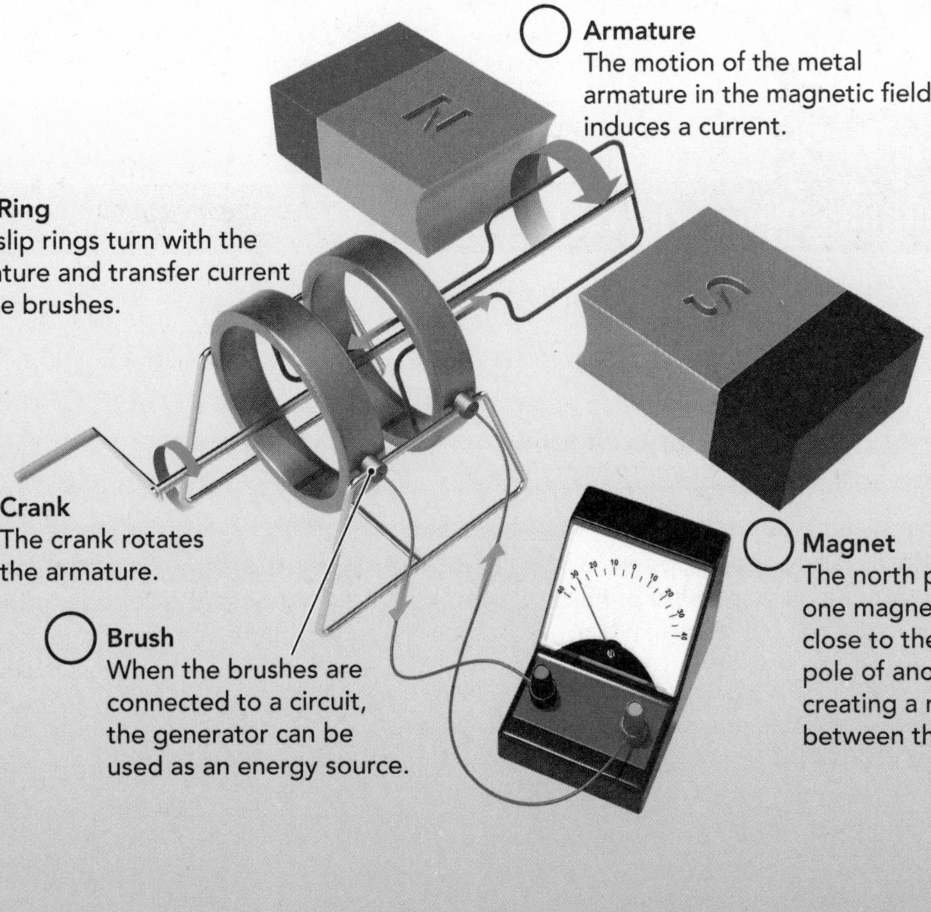

○ **Armature**
The motion of the metal armature in the magnetic field induces a current.

○ **Slip Ring**
The slip rings turn with the armature and transfer current to the brushes.

○ **Crank**
The crank rotates the armature.

○ **Brush**
When the brushes are connected to a circuit, the generator can be used as an energy source.

○ **Magnet**
The north pole of one magnet is placed close to the south pole of another magnet, creating a magnetic field between them.

Step-Up Transformer

Step-Down Transformer

Types of Transformers

Figure 10 In step-up transformers, the primary coil has fewer loops than the secondary coil. In step-down transformers, the primary coil has more loops.

How Transformers Work You have probably heard the word *transformer* before. What does it mean when a transformer refers to electric current? This type of **transformer** is a device that increases or decreases voltage using two separate coils of insulated wire that are wrapped around an iron core.

The first coil that the current goes through is called the primary coil. This coil is connected to a circuit with a voltage source and alternating current. The other coil is called the secondary coil. It is connected to a circuit, but it does not have a voltage source. The coils share an iron core. Because the primary coil is connected to alternating current, the direction of the current constantly changes. As a result, the magnetic field around it also changes, and it induces a current in the secondary coil.

There are two types of transformers. As shown in **Figure 10**, the type depends on which coil has more loops. Step-up transformers, such as those used to help transmit electricity from generating plants, increase voltage. Step-down transformers, such as those used in phone chargers, decrease voltage. The phone charger plugs into an outlet and reduces the voltage to what is needed to charge a cell phone. The greater the difference between the number of loops in the primary and secondary coils in a transformer, the more the voltage will change.

✓ READING CHECK **Summarize Text** How are generators and transformers related?

....

....

Math Toolbox

Voltage Change in Transformers

The equation shows that the ratio of voltage in the two coils is equal to the ratio of loops.

$$\frac{\text{primary voltage}}{\text{secondary voltage}} = \frac{\text{primary loops}}{\text{secondary loops}}$$

1. Understand Ratio Concepts Suppose a step-up transformer has 1 loop in the primary coil and 8 loops in the secondary coil. If the secondary voltage is 120 V, what must be the primary voltage? Show your work.

....

....

2. Reason Quantitatively In a step-down transformer, suppose the voltage in the primary coil is 600 V and the voltage in the secondary coil is 150 V. If there are 36 loops in the primary coil, how many loops are in the secondary coil?

....

....

☑LESSON 4 Check

MS-PS2-3

1. Calculate What will be the primary voltage of a transformer if the secondary voltage is 60 V and there are 40 loops on the primary coil and 120 loops on the secondary coil? Show your work.

2. Compare and Contrast How are electric motors and generators similar? How are they different?

....

....

....

....

....

....

....

3. Construct an Explanation In many areas electricity is produced by big generators within dams. What function does large volumes of moving water have in generating electricity?

....

....

....

....

....

4. Apply Scientific Reasoning Suppose you build model airplanes. Use what you know from this lesson to draw a model of a device that would keep a propeller turning as the plane flew.

In this lesson, you discovered how an electric charge in motion experiences a magnetic force in a magnetic field. You also learned how charges can be set in motion within a conductor by moving the conductor through a magnetic field. A moving magnetic field can also induce a current through a wire. Additionally, you discovered how motors, generators, and transformers work.

Apply Concepts How might a motor, generator, or transformer be used as part of your levitation device?

....

....

....

HANDS-ON LAB

Electrifying Levitation

Go online to download the lab worksheet. Test your levitation device and see how an optimal design can be achieved.

This is an artist's conception of the X-57 Maxwell, showing the electric motors on the extra-thin wings.

THE X-57 Maxwell

Airplanes fly people, mail, and cargo all over the world. Fossil fuels supply the power that planes need in order to fly. With the reserves of fossil fuels dropping, engineers and scientists continue to look for alternative sources of power for planes and other forms of transportation.

NASA's X-57 Maxwell, which is nearing the completion of a long development process, has proved that a battery-powered plane is a possibility. NASA engineers nicknamed the plane "Maxwell" in honor of Scottish physicist James Clerk Maxwell, whose discoveries in physics rank him right behind Einstein and Newton.

The X-57 won't just have electric motors instead of engines; it will have many design features that distinguish it from a traditional plane. The wings will be much smaller, which will reduce the plane's weight and wind resistance. The electric motors will weigh about half as much as traditional combustion engines, and there will be fourteen of them instead of one or two. Twelve of the motors will shut down once the plane is at cruising altitude. There will be special design elements to reduce drag while the plane is aloft.

There are disadvantages to the battery-propelled plane, however. Because the batteries are heavy, the plane won't be able to carry much weight, or many passengers. The plane would also fly more slowly than fuel-power planes, and have a flight distance of about 160 kilometers before its batteries would have to be recharged.

Still, a battery-propelled plane would have many advantages over one that is powered by fossil fuels. Generating the electricity to power the batteries could release less carbon dioxide, which is good news for the climate. Electric motors would also make far less noise than traditional combustion engines.

	X-57 Maxwell	Combustion-Engine Version of Same Plane
Aircraft Weight	1360 kg	819 kg
Cruising Speed	277 km/h	278 km/h
Takeoff Speed	109 km/h	65 km/h
Range	160 km	1240 km

Use the text and the data table to answer the following questions.

1. Summarize Describe the physical features that will make the X-57 Maxwell unique.

   ....

   ....

   ....

2. Calculate What fraction of the plane's full speed would be needed for the plane to get off the ground?

   ....

   ....

3. Evaluate What factor, aside from the reliance on a battery, do you think makes the range of the X-57 Maxwell shorter than the range of the combustion-engine version of the same plane?

   ....

   ....

4. Apply Concepts Suppose that the technology pioneered by the X-57 were applied to passenger airliners. What is one advantage that passengers would experience by flying on an X-57 instead of a traditional combustion-engine plane? What would be one disadvantage of passengers flying on an X-57?

   ....

   ....

1 Electric Force

MS-PS2-5, MS-PS3-2

1. The area around a charge in which the electric force is experienced by other charged objects is the
   A. electric charge.   B. electric field.
   C. electric force.   D. electric current.

2. Charges flow through a circuit due to differences in
   A. resistance.   B. potential energy.
   C. conductivity.   D. insulation.

3. Why would two electrons repel each other if they were close together?
   A. They have like charges, so they experience an attractive force.
   B. They have opposite charges, so they experience a repulsive force.
   C. They have like charges, so they experience a repulsive force.
   D. They have opposite charges, so they experience an attractive force.

4. In ...., current flows more easily because electrons are more loosely bound to their atoms than they are in insulators.

5. **Construct Explanations** Suppose a blanket has a sock stuck to it due to static electricity. When you pull the sock off of the blanket, what happens to the potential energy between them? Explain your response.

....

....

....

....

....

....

2 Magnetic Force

MS-PS2-5, MS-PS3-2

6. The push or pull that occurs when a magnet interacts with another object is known as the
   A. magnetic force.   B. magnetic field.
   C. magnetism.   D. magnet.

7. How is a magnet able to pick up bits of metal without actually touching them?
   A. The magnet is surrounded by an electric field that attracts the metal.
   B. The metal exerts a repulsive force on the magnet.
   C. There is an invisible magnetic field around the magnet where it exerts magnetic force.
   D. The electric force from the magnet attracts the bits of metal.

8. **Explain Phenomena** A magnet is placed on a refrigerator to hold up a calendar. As the magnet approaches the refrigerator, the potential energy between the magnet and the refrigerator decreases. Explain why.

....

....

....

....

....

9. **Develop Models** Draw the magnetic field lines around a bar magnet, and label the places where the magnetic field is the strongest.

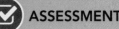
3 Electromagnetic Force

MS-PS2-3

10. What do you call the relationship between electricity and magnetism?

A. static electricity   B. magnetic current

C. electric force   D. electromagnetism

11. A(n) .... is a coil of wire with a current running through it. If you wrap the coil around a ferromagnetic material, it becomes a(n) ....

12. Use Models In the diagram, the direction of a current and the magnetic field around it are shown. Describe what would happen to the magnetic field if you increased the number of turns in the coil and reversed the direction of the current.

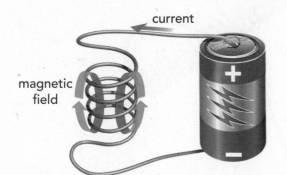

current

magnetic field

....

....

....

....

....

....

....

....

4 Electric and Magnetic interactions

MS-PS2-3

13. Which of the following descriptions describes electromagnetic induction?

A. Current running through a wire creates a magnetic field.

B. Moving a conductor through a magnetic field generates a current through the conductor.

C. Connecting a conductive wire to both ends of a battery allows current to flow.

D. Moving north poles of two magnets away from each other decreases potential energy.

14. A step-down transformer has a voltage of 400 V through the primary coil and 200 V through the secondary coil. There are 5 loops in the secondary coil. How many loops are in the primary coil?

A. 2 loops   B. 5 loops

C. 10 loops   D. 20 loops

15. Increasing the number of magnets within an electric motor will .... (increase/decrease) the speed of the motor.

16. Determine Differences Electric motors and generators have similar parts but are considered to be opposites. Describe how they are different in terms of electromagnetism and the transformations of energy involved.

....

....

....

....

....

....

....

....

MS-PS2-3, MS-PS2-5, MS-PS3-2

Evidence-Based Assessment

Manny is investigating factors that affect electric and magnetic forces. He needs to design an experiment to show that objects can exert forces on each other even when they are not in direct contact.

After doing some additional research, Manny decides to make an electromagnet with a battery, some wire, an iron nail, and a switch. He uses a rubber eraser as an insulator to open and close the switch. He uses the electromagnet to see if he can pick up some paperclips.

The diagram shows the setup of Manny's experiment.

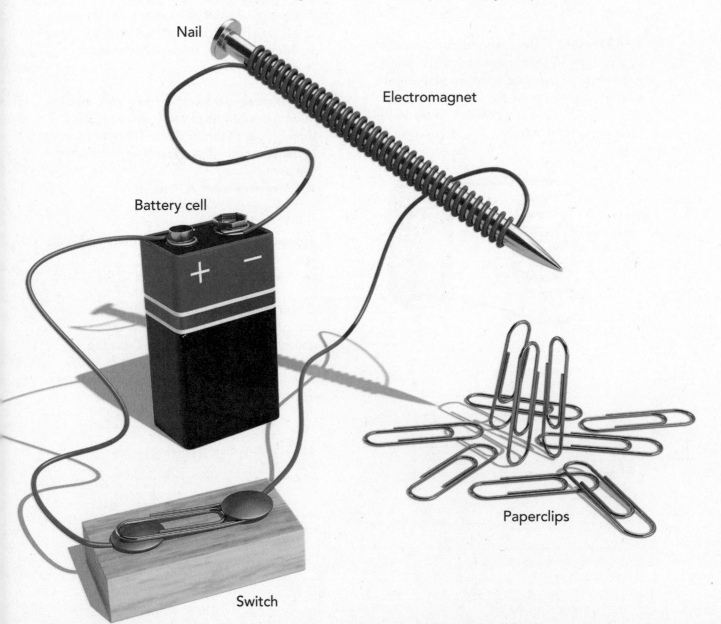

Nail

Electromagnet

Battery cell

Paperclips

Switch

1. **Analyze Data** What is one of the benefits of Manny's electromagnet?
   A. It can only repel objects.
   B. It produces a current through electromagnetic induction.
   C. The magnetic field can be turned on and off.
   D. Its strength cannot be changed.

2. **Cause and Effect** What could Manny do to increase the strength of the electromagnetic force? Select all that apply.
   ☐ Increase the number of coils around the nail.
   ☐ Increase the current by using a battery with a greater voltage.
   ☐ Decrease the number of coils around the nail.
   ☐ Decrease the current by using a battery with a smaller voltage.

3. **Cite Evidence** What evidence is there that the electromagnet exerts a force on the paper clips, even though they are not touching each other?

   ....
   ....
   ....
   ....
   ....

4. **Analyze Systems** Manny detaches the two wires from the battery and reattaches them to the opposite terminals. Explain how this changes the current and magnetic field.

   ....
   ....
   ....
   ....
   ....
   ....

5. **Explain Phenomena** Suppose you pull the paperclips away from the nail. Explain how the potential energy between the paperclips and the nail changes.

   ....
   ....
   ....
   ....
   ....
   ....
   ....
   ....

Quest FINDINGS

Complete the Quest!

Phenomenon Reflect on the engineering and design work you did building your levitating device.

Connect to Technology Magnets are used in a variety of industrial and medical applications. How do you think magnet technology might be applied to sports?

....
....
....
....

INTERACTIVITY

Reflect on Your Levitating Device

Planetary Detective

How can you **build** a device to **detect** magnetic fields on distant planets?

Background

A group of astronomers has approached you for assistance. They are studying three exoplanets, or planets that orbit a star outside our solar system. The three planets orbit in the habitable zone of the star. This means that liquid water can potentially exist on the planets, which is one requirement for life as we know it. The astronomers want to know whether or not the planets have magnetic fields, which will help them determine each planet's capacity for supporting life.

In this investigation, you will build a simple magnetometer, a device that detects magnetic fields, to test models of the three planets. Using evidence from your investigation, you will decide which of the planets have magnetic fields and which one most likely could support life.

Materials

(per pair)

- 3 planet models
- iron filings, 50 mL
- paper cups, 2–3
- pieces of cardboard or small cardboard box
- string, 60 cm
- clear tape
- scissors
- plastic wrap, 2–3 sheets
- copy paper, 3–4 sheets
- small bar magnet

Safety

Be sure to follow all safety guidelines provided by your teacher. The Safety Appendix of your textbook provides more details about the safety icons.

Earth's magnetic field helps to deflect charged particles in dangerous solar wind. Without this magnetic field, life would not be possible on our planet.

Design Your Investigation

1. In your investigation, you must build a magnetometer and use it to look for evidence of magnetic fields for models of the three exoplanets, provided by your teacher. Space probes and satellites use this technology to look for evidence of magnetic fields and metals on planets throughout our solar system without coming into contact with the planets.

2. Think about how you can use the available materials to build a magnetometer. Consider the following questions as you work with your group to design your device:

   - How can you use the iron filings to help you detect and observe magnetic forces?

   - How can you use the cups or cardboard along with paper or plastic wrap to design a device that keep the iron filings contained and allows you to safely observe them?

   - How can you make sure that your device's design allows it to detect magnetic fields without coming into contact with the model?

   - How can you use the magnet to test your device?

3. Sketch your design in the space provided and be sure to label the materials you are using to construct the magnetometer. Then build your device.

4. Plan your investigation by determining how you will use the magnetometer to test the models. Record your plan in the space provided. Consider the following questions as you develop your plan:

   - How can you determine whether or not the planet you are studying has a magnetic field?

   - If you detect magnetic fields, how can you compare the strength of the planets' magnetic forces?

5. After getting your teacher's approval, carry out your investigation. Make a table to record your observations and data in the space provided.

Sketch and Procedure

Data Table and Observations

Analyze and Interpret Data

1. **Apply Concepts** What characteristics do you think a planet needs in order to generate a magnetic field?

....

....

....

....

2. **Use Models** Look at your data and observations for the planet with the strongest magnetic field. The iron filings in your magnetometer were attracted to the magnetic material inside the model. Where does the greatest amount of potential energy exist—when the magnetometer is 10 cm from the surface of the planet or when the magnetometer is 3 cm the surface of the planet? Explain.

....

....

....

....

....

3. **Cause and Effect** How do the results of your investigation provide evidence that the magnetic force inside the planet interacts with the iron filings in the magnetometer even though they do not come into contact with each other?

....

....

....

....

4. **Construct Arguments** Which of the three planets most likely could support life? Support your response with evidence from your investigation.

....

....

....

....

....

SEP.1, SEP.8

The Meaning of Science

Science Skills

Reflect Think about a time you misplaced something and could not find it. Write a sentence defining the problem. What science skills could you use to solve the problem? Explain how you would use at least three of the skills in the table.

Science is a way of learning about the natural world. It involves asking questions, making predictions, and collecting information to see if the answer is right or wrong.

The table lists some of the skills that scientists use. You use some of these skills every day. For example, you may observe and evaluate your lunch options before choosing what to eat.

Skill	Definition
classifying	grouping together items that are alike or that have shared characteristics
evaluating	comparing observations and data to reach a conclusion
inferring	explaining or interpreting observations
investigating	studying or researching a subject to discover facts or to reveal new information
making models	creating representations of complex objects or processes
observing	using one or more of your senses to gather information
predicting	making a statement or claim about what will happen based on past experience or evidence

Scientific Attitudes

Curiosity often drives scientists to learn about the world around them. Creativity is useful for coming up with inventive ways to solve problems. Such qualities and attitudes, and the ability to keep an open mind, are essential for scientists.

When sharing results or findings, honesty and ethics are also essential. Ethics refers to rules for knowing right from wrong.

Being skeptical is also important. This means having doubts about things based on past experiences and evidence. Skepticism helps to prevent accepting data and results that may not be true.

Scientists must also avoid bias—likes or dislikes of people, ideas, or things. They must avoid experimental bias, which is a mistake that may make an experiment's preferred outcome more likely.

Scientific Reasoning

Scientific reasoning depends on being logical and objective. When you are objective, you use evidence and apply logic to draw conclusions. Being subjective means basing conclusions on personal feelings, biases, or opinions. Subjective reasoning can interfere with science and skew results. Objective reasoning helps scientists use observations to reach conclusions about the natural world.

Scientists use two types of objective reasoning: deductive and inductive. Deductive reasoning involves starting with a general idea or theory and applying it to a situation. For example, the theory of plate tectonics indicates that earthquakes happen mostly where tectonic plates meet. You could then draw the conclusion, or deduce, that California has many earthquakes because tectonic plates meet there.

In inductive reasoning, you make a generalization from a specific observation. When scientists collect data in an experiment and draw a conclusion based on that data, they use inductive reasoning. For example, if fertilizer causes one set of plants to grow faster than another, you might infer that the fertilizer promotes plant growth.

Make Meaning
Think about a bias the marine biologist in the photo could show that results in paying more or less attention to one kind of organism over others. Make a prediction about how that bias could affect the biologist's survey of the coral reef.

Write About It
Suppose it is raining when you go to sleep one night. When you wake up the next morning, you observe frozen puddles on the ground and icicles on tree branches. Use scientific reasoning to draw a conclusion about the air temperature outside. Support your conclusion using deductive or inductive reasoning.

SEP.1, SEP.2, SEP.3, SEP.4, CCC.4

Science Processes

Scientific Inquiry

Write About It
Describe a question that you posed, formally or informally, about an event in your life that you needed to investigate or resolve. Write the hypothesis you developed to answer your question, and describe how you tested the hypothesis.

Scientists contribute to scientific knowledge by conducting investigations and drawing conclusions. The process often begins with an observation that leads to a question, which is then followed by the development of a hypothesis. This is known as scientific inquiry.

One of the first steps in scientific inquiry is asking questions. However, it's important to make a question specific with a narrow focus so the investigation will not be too broad. A biologist may want to know all there is to know about wolves, for example. But a good, focused question for a specific inquiry might be "How many offspring does the average female wolf produce in her lifetime?"

A hypothesis is a possible answer to a scientific question. A hypothesis must be testable. For something to be testable, researchers must be able to carry out an investigation and gather evidence that will either support or disprove the hypothesis.

Scientific Models

Models are tools that scientists use to study phenomena indirectly. A model is any representation of an object or process. Illustrations, dioramas, globes, diagrams, computer programs, and mathematical equations are all examples of scientific models. For example, a diagram of Earth's crust and mantle can help you to picture layers deep below the surface and understand events such as volcanic eruptions.

Models also allow scientists to represent objects that are either very large, such as our solar system, or very small, such as a molecule of DNA. Models can also represent processes that occur over a long period of time, such as the changes that have occurred throughout Earth's history.

Models are helpful, but they have limitations. Physical models are not made of the same materials as the objects they represent. Most models of complex objects or processes show only major parts, stages, or relationships. Many details are left out. Therefore, you may not be able to learn as much from models as you would through direct observation.

Reflect Identify the benefits and limitations of using a plastic model of DNA, as shown here.

Science Experiments

An experiment or investigation must be well planned to produce valid results. In planning an experiment, you must identify the independent and dependent variables. You must also do as much as possible to remove the effects of other variables. A controlled experiment is one in which you test only one variable at a time.

For example, suppose you plan a controlled experiment to learn how the type of material affects the speed at which sound waves travel through it. The only variable that should change is the type of material. This way, if the speed of sound changes, you know that it is a result of a change in the material, not another variable such as the thickness of the material or the type of sound used.

You should also remove bias from any investigation. You may inadvertently introduce bias by selecting subjects you like and avoiding those you don't like. Scientists often conduct investigations by taking random samples to avoid ending up with biased results.

Once you plan your investigation and begin to collect data, it's important to record and organize the data. You may wish to use a graph to display and help you to interpret the data.

Communicating is the sharing of ideas and results with others through writing and speaking. Communicating data and conclusions is a central part of science.

Scientists share knowledge, including new findings, theories, and techniques for collecting data. Conferences, journals, and websites help scientists to communicate with each other. Popular media, including newspapers, magazines, and social media sites, help scientists to share their knowledge with nonscientists. However, before the results of investigations are shared and published, other scientists should review the experiment for possible sources of error, such as bias and unsupported conclusions.

Write About It
List four ways you could communicate the results of a scientific study about the health of sea turtles in the Pacific Ocean.

SEP.1, SEP.6, SEP.7, SEP.8

Scientific Knowledge

Scientific Explanations

Suppose you learn that adult flamingos are pink because of the food they eat. This statement is a scientific explanation— it describes how something in nature works or explains why it happens. Scientists from different fields use methods such as researching information, designing experiments, and making models to form scientific explanations. Scientific explanations often result from many years of work and multiple investigations conducted by many scientists.

Scientific Theories and Laws

A scientific law is a statement that describes what you can expect to occur every time under a particular set of conditions. A scientific law describes an observed pattern in nature, but it does not attempt to explain it. For example, the law of superposition describes what you can expect to find in terms of the ages of layers of rock. Geologists use this observed pattern to determine the relative ages of sedimentary rock layers. But the law does not explain why the pattern occurs.

By contrast, a scientific theory is a well-tested explanation for a wide range of observations or experimental results. It provides details and describes causes of observed patterns. Something is elevated to a theory only when there is a large body of evidence that supports it. However, a scientific theory can be changed or overturned when new evidence is found.

Write About It
Choose two fields of science that interest you. Describe a method used to develop scientific explanations in each field.

Compare and Contrast Complete the table to compare and contrast a scientific theory and a scientific law.

	Scientific Theory	Scientific Law
Definition		
Does it attempt to explain a pattern observed in nature?		

Analyzing Scientific Explanations

To analyze scientific explanations that you hear on the news or read in a book such as this one, you need scientific literacy. Scientific literacy means understanding scientific terms and principles well enough to ask questions, evaluate information, and make decisions. Scientific reasoning gives you a process to apply. This includes looking for bias and errors in the research, evaluating data, and identifying faulty reasoning. For example, by evaluating how a survey was conducted, you may find a serious flaw in the researchers' methods.

Evidence and Opinions

The basis for scientific explanations is empirical evidence. Empirical evidence includes the data and observations that have been collected through scientific processes. Satellite images, photos, and maps of mountains and volcanoes are all examples of empirical evidence that support a scientific explanation about Earth's tectonic plates. Scientists look for patterns when they analyze this evidence. For example, they might see a pattern that mountains and volcanoes often occur near tectonic plate boundaries.

To evaluate scientific information, you must first distinguish between evidence and opinion. In science, evidence includes objective observations and conclusions that have been repeated. Evidence may or may not support a scientific claim. An opinion is a subjective idea that is formed from evidence, but it cannot be confirmed by evidence.

Write About It
Suppose the conservation committee of a town wants to gauge residents' opinions about a proposal to stock the local ponds with fish every spring. The committee pays for a survey to appear on a web site that is popular with people who like to fish. The results of the survey show 78 people in favor of the proposal and two against it. Do you think the survey's results are valid? Explain.

Make Meaning
Explain what empirical evidence the photograph reveals.

SEP.3, SEP.4

Tools of Science

Measurement

Making measurements using standard units is important in all fields of science. This allows scientists to repeat and reproduce other experiments, as well as to understand the precise meaning of the results of others. Scientists use a measurement system called the International System of Units, or SI.

For each type of measurement, there is a series of units that are greater or less than each other. The unit a scientist uses depends on what is being measured. For example, a geophysicist tracking the movements of tectonic plates may use centimeters, as plates tend to move small amounts each year. Meanwhile, a marine biologist might measure the movement of migrating bluefin tuna on the scale of kilometers.

Units for length, mass, volume, and density are based on powers of ten—a meter is equal to 100 centimeters or 1000 millimeters. Units of time do not follow that pattern. There are 60 seconds in a minute, 60 minutes in an hour, and 24 hours in a day. These units are based on patterns that humans perceived in nature. Units of temperature are based on scales that are set according to observations of nature. For example, 0°C is the temperature at which pure water freezes, and 100°C is the temperature at which it boils.

Write About It
Suppose you are planning an investigation in which you must measure the dimensions of several small mineral samples that fit in your hand. Which metric unit or units will you most likely use? Explain your answer.

Measurement	Metric units
Length or distance	meter (m), kilometer (km), centimeter (cm), millimeter (mm) 1 km = 1,000 m 1 cm = 10 mm 1 m = 100 cm
Mass	kilogram (kg), gram (g), milligram (mg) 1 kg = 1,000 g 1 g = 1,000 mg
Volume	cubic meter (m^3), cubic centimeter (cm^3) 1 m^3 = 1,000,000 cm^3
Density	kilogram per cubic meter (kg/m^3), gram per cubic centimeter (g/cm^3) 1,000 kg/m^3 = 1 g/cm^3
Temperature	degrees Celsius (°C), kelvin (K) 1°C = 273 K
Time	hour (h), minute (m), second (s)

Math Skills

Using numbers to collect and interpret data involves math skills that are essential in science. For example, you use math skills when you estimate the number of birds in an entire forest after counting the actual number of birds in ten trees.

Scientists evaluate measurements and estimates for their precision and accuracy. In science, an accurate measurement is very close to the actual value. Precise measurements are very close, or nearly equal, to each other. Reliable measurements are both accurate and precise. An imprecise value may be a sign of an error in data collection. This kind of anomalous data may be excluded to avoid skewing the data and harming the investigation.

Other math skills include performing specific calculations, such as finding the mean, or average, value in a data set. The mean can be calculated by adding up all of the values in the data set and then dividing that sum by the number of values.

Hour	Number of Ducks Observed at a Pond
1	12
2	10
3	2
4	14
5	13
6	10
7	11

Calculate The data table shows how many ducks were seen at a pond every hour over the course of seven hours. Is there a data point that seems anomalous? If so, cross out that data point. Then, calculate the mean number of ducks on the pond. Round the mean to the nearest whole number.

....

Graphs

Graphs help scientists to interpret data by helping them to find trends or patterns in the data. A line graph displays data that show how one variable (the dependent or outcome variable) changes in response to another (the independent or test variable). The slope and shape of a graph line can reveal patterns and help scientists to make predictions. For example, line graphs can help you to spot patterns of change over time.

Scientists use bar graphs to compare data across categories or subjects that may not affect each other. The heights of the bars make it easy to compare those quantities. A circle graph, also known as a pie chart, shows the proportions of different parts of a whole.

Write About It
You and a friend record the distance you travel every 15 minutes on a one-hour bike trip. Your friend wants to display the data as a circle graph. Explain whether or not this is the best type of graph to display your data. If not, suggest another graph to use.

SEP.1, SEP.2, SEP.3, SEP.6

The Engineering and Design Process

Engineers are builders and problem solvers. Chemical engineers experiment with new fuels made from algae. Civil engineers design roadways and bridges. Bioengineers develop medical devices and prosthetics. The common trait among engineers is an ability to identify problems and design solutions to solve them. Engineers use a creative process that relies on scientific methods to help guide them from a concept or idea all the way to the final product.

Define the Problem

To identify or define a problem, different questions need to be asked: *What are the effects of the problem? What are the likely causes? What other factors could be involved?* Sometimes the obvious, immediate cause of a problem may be the result of another problem that may not be immediately apparent. For example, climate change results in different weather patterns, which in turn can affect organisms that live in certain habitats. So engineers must be aware of all the possible effects of potential solutions. Engineers must also take into account how well different solutions deal with the different causes of the problem.

Reflect Write about a problem that you encountered in your life that had both immediate, obvious causes as well as less-obvious and less-immediate ones.

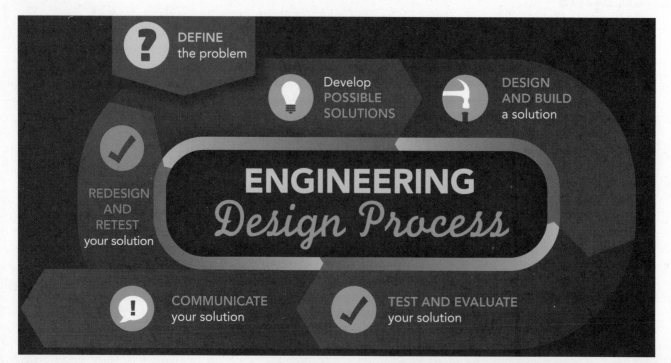

ENGINEERING *Design Process*

DEFINE the problem

Develop POSSIBLE SOLUTIONS

DESIGN AND BUILD a solution

REDESIGN AND RETEST your solution

COMMUNICATE your solution

TEST AND EVALUATE your solution

As engineers consider problems and design solutions, they must identify and categorize the criteria and constraints of the project.

Criteria are the factors that must be met or accomplished by the solution. For example, a gardener who wants to protect outdoor plants from deer and rabbits may say that the criteria for the solution are "plants are no longer eaten" and "plant growth is not inhibited in any way." The gardener then knows the plants cannot simply be sealed off from the environment, because the plants will not receive sunlight and water.

The same gardener will likely have constraints on his solution, such as budget for materials and time that is available for working on the project. By setting constraints, a solution can be designed that will be successful without introducing a new set of problems. No one wants to spend $500 on materials to protect $100 worth of tomatoes and cucumbers.

Develop Possible Solutions

After the problem has been identified, and the criteria and constraints identified, an engineer will consider possible solutions. This often involves working in teams with other engineers and designers to brainstorm ideas and research materials that can be used in the design.

It's important for engineers to think creatively and explore all potential solutions. If you wanted to design a bicycle that was safer and easier to ride than a traditional bicycle, then you would want more than just one or two solutions. Having multiple ideas to choose from increases the likelihood that you will develop a solution that meets the criteria and constraints. In addition, different ideas that result from brainstorming can often lead to new and better solutions to an existing problem.

Make Meaning
Using the example of a garden that is vulnerable to wild animals such as deer, make a list of likely constraints on an engineering solution to the problem you identified before. Determine if there are common traits among the constraints, and identify categories for them.

Design a Solution

Engineers then develop the idea that they feel best solves the problem. Once a solution has been chosen, engineers and designers get to work building a model or prototype of the solution. A model may involve sketching on paper or using computer software to construct a model of the solution. A prototype is a working model of the solution.

Building a model or prototype helps an engineer determine whether a solution meets the criteria and stays within the constraints. During this stage of the process, engineers must often deal with new problems and make any necessary adjustments to the model or prototype.

Test and Evaluate a Solution

Whether testing a model or a prototype, engineers use scientific processes to evaluate their solutions. Multiple experiments, tests, or trials are conducted, data are evaluated, and results and analyses are communicated. New criteria or constraints may emerge as a result of testing. In most cases, a solution will require some refinement or revision, even if it has been through successful testing. Refining a solution is necessary if there are new constraints, such as less money or available materials. Additional testing may be done to ensure that a solution satisfies local, state, or federal laws or standards.

Make Meaning Think about an aluminum beverage can. What would happen if the price or availability of aluminum changed so much that cans needed to be made of a new material? What would the criteria and constraints be on the development of a new can?

A naval architect sets up a model to test how the the hull's design responds to waves.

Communicate the Solution

Engineers need to communicate the final design to the people who will manufacture the product. This may include sketches, detailed drawings, computer simulations, and written text. Engineers often provide evidence that was collected during the testing stage. This evidence may include graphs and data tables that support the decisions made for the final design.

If there is feedback about the solution, then the engineers and designers must further refine the solution. This might involve making minor adjustments to the design, or it might mean bigger modifications to the design based on new criteria or constraints. Any changes in the design will require additional testing to make sure that the changes work as intended.

Redesign and Retest the Solution

At different steps in the engineering and design process, a solution usually must be revised and retested. Many designs fail to work perfectly, even after models and prototypes are built, tested, and evaluated. Engineers must be ready to analyze new results and deal with any new problems that arise. Troubleshooting, or fixing design problems, allows engineers to adjust the design to improve on how well the solution meets the need.

Communicate Suppose you are an engineer at an aerospace company. Your team is designing a rover to be used on a future NASA space mission. A family member doesn't understand why so much your team's time is taken up with testing and retesting the rover design. What are three things you would tell your relative to explain why testing and retesting are so important to the engineering and design process?

....

....

....

....

....

....

....

....

APPENDIX A

Safety Symbols

These symbols warn of possible dangers in the laboratory and remind you to work carefully.

Safety Goggles Wear safety goggles to protect your eyes in any activity involving chemicals, flames or heating, or glassware.

Lab Apron Wear a laboratory apron to protect your skin and clothing from damage.

Breakage Handle breakable materials, such as glassware, with care. Do not touch broken glassware.

Heat-Resistant Gloves Use an oven mitt or other hand protection when handling hot materials, such as hot plates or hot glassware.

Plastic Gloves Wear disposable plastic gloves when working with harmful chemicals and organisms. Keep your hands away from your face, and dispose of the gloves according to your teacher's instructions.

Heating Use a clamp or tongs to pick up hot glassware. Do not touch hot objects with your bare hands.

Flames Before you work with flames, tie back loose hair and clothing. Follow your teacher's instructions about lighting and extinguishing flames.

No Flames When using flammable materials, make sure there are no flames, sparks, or other exposed heat sources present.

Corrosive Chemical Avoid getting acid or other corrosive chemicals on your skin or clothing or in your eyes. Do not inhale the vapors. Wash your hands after the activity.

Poison Do not let any poisonous chemical come into contact with your skin, and do not inhale its vapors. Wash your hands when you are finished with the activity.

Fumes Work in a well-ventilated area when harmful vapors may be involved. Avoid inhaling vapors directly. Test an odor only when directed to do so by your teacher, and use a wafting motion to direct the vapor toward your nose.

Sharp Object Scissors, scalpels, knives, needles, pins, and tacks can cut your skin. Always direct a sharp edge or point away from yourself and others.

Animal Safety Treat live or preserved animals or animal parts with care to avoid harming the animals or yourself. Wash your hands when you are finished with the activity.

Plant Safety Handle plants only as directed by your teacher. If you are allergic to certain plants, tell your teacher; do not do an activity involving those plants. Avoid touching harmful plants such as poison ivy. Wash your hands when you are finished with the activity.

Electric Shock To avoid electric shock, never use electrical equipment around water, when the equipment is wet, or when your hands are wet. Be sure cords are untangled and cannot trip anyone. Unplug equipment not in use.

Physical Safety When an experiment involves physical activity, avoid injuring yourself or others. Alert your teacher if there is any reason you should not participate.

Disposal Dispose of chemicals and other laboratory materials safely. Follow the instructions from your teacher.

Hand Washing Wash your hands thoroughly when finished with an activity. Use soap and warm water. Rinse well.

General Safety Awareness When this symbol appears, follow the instructions provided. When you are asked to develop your own procedure in a lab, have your teacher approve your plan.

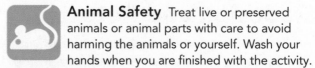

Using a Laboratory Balance

The laboratory balance is an important tool in scientific investigations. Different kinds of balances are used in the laboratory to determine the masses and weights of objects. You can use a triple-beam balance to determine the masses of materials that you study or experiment with in the laboratory. An electronic balance, unlike a triple-beam balance, is used to measure the weights of materials.

The triple-beam balance that you may use in your science class is probably similar to the balance depicted in this Appendix. To use the balance properly, you should learn the name, location, and function of each part of the balance.

Triple-Beam Balance

The triple-beam balance is a single-pan balance with three beams calibrated in grams. The back, or 100-gram, beam is divided into ten units of 10 grams each. The middle, or 500-gram, beam is divided into five units of 100 grams each. The front, or 10-gram, beam is divided into ten units of 1 gram each. Each gram on the front beam is further divided into units of 0.1 gram.

Apply Concepts What is the greatest mass you could find with the triple-beam balance in the picture?

....

Calculate What is the mass of the apple in the picture?

....

The following procedure can be used to find the mass of an object with a triple-beam balance:

1. Place the object on the pan.

2. Move the rider on the middle beam notch by notch until the horizontal pointer on the right drops below zero. Move the rider back one notch.

3. Move the rider on the back beam notch by notch until the pointer again drops below zero. Move the rider back one notch.

4. Slowly slide the rider along the front beam until the pointer stops at the zero point.

5. The mass of the object is equal to the sum of the readings on the three beams.

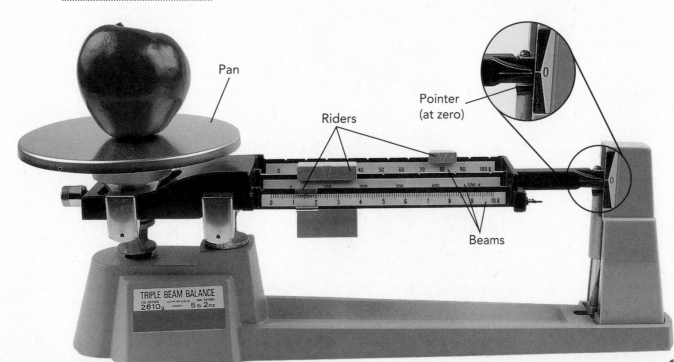

Pan

Riders

Pointer (at zero)

Beams

TRIPLE BEAM BALANCE
700 SERIES   U.S. PAT. NO. 2,275,418   800 SERIES
2610g   CAPACITY   5 lb 2 oz

Using a Microscope

The microscope is an essential tool in the study of life science. It allows you to see things that are too small to be seen with the unaided eye.

You will probably use a compound microscope like the one you see here. The compound microscope has more than one lens that magnifies the object you view.

Typically, a compound microscope has one lens in the eyepiece (the part you look through). The eyepiece lens usually magnifies 10×. Any object you view through this lens will appear 10 times larger than it is.

A compound microscope may contain two or three other lenses called objective lenses. They are called the low-power and high-power objective lenses. The low-power objective lens usually magnifies 10×. The high-power objective lenses usually magnify 40× and 100×.

To calculate the total magnification with which you are viewing an object, multiply the magnification of the eyepiece lens by the magnification of the objective lens you are using. For example, the eyepiece's magnification of 10× multiplied by the low-power objective's magnification of 10× equals a total magnification of 100×.

Use the photo of the compound microscope to become familiar with the parts of the microscope and their functions.

The Parts of a Microscope

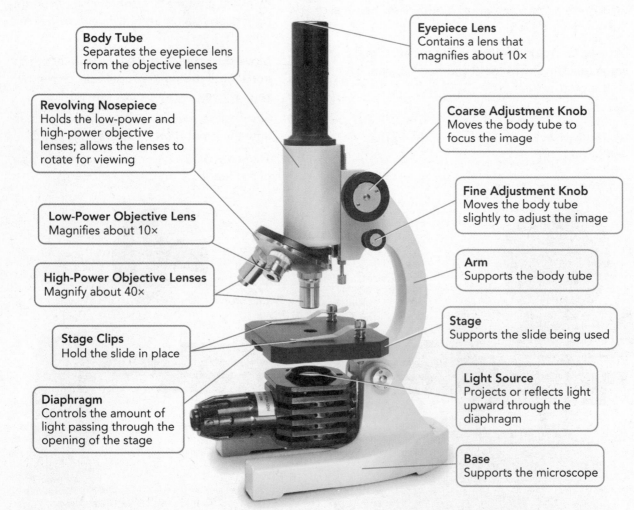

Body Tube
Separates the eyepiece lens from the objective lenses

Revolving Nosepiece
Holds the low-power and high-power objective lenses; allows the lenses to rotate for viewing

Low-Power Objective Lens
Magnifies about 10×

High-Power Objective Lenses
Magnify about 40×

Stage Clips
Hold the slide in place

Diaphragm
Controls the amount of light passing through the opening of the stage

Eyepiece Lens
Contains a lens that magnifies about 10×

Coarse Adjustment Knob
Moves the body tube to focus the image

Fine Adjustment Knob
Moves the body tube slightly to adjust the image

Arm
Supports the body tube

Stage
Supports the slide being used

Light Source
Projects or reflects light upward through the diaphragm

Base
Supports the microscope

Using the Microscope

Use the following procedures when you are working with a microscope.

1. To carry the microscope, grasp the microscope's arm with one hand. Place your other hand under the base.

2. Place the microscope on a table with the arm toward you.

3. Turn the coarse adjustment knob to raise the body tube.

4. Revolve the nosepiece until the low-power objective lens clicks into place.

5. Adjust the diaphragm. While looking through the eyepiece, adjust the mirror until you see a bright white circle of light. **CAUTION:** Never use direct sunlight as a light source.

6. Place a slide on the stage. Center the specimen over the opening on the stage. Use the stage clips to hold the slide in place. **CAUTION:** Glass slides are fragile.

7. Look at the stage from the side. Carefully turn the coarse adjustment knob to lower the body tube until the low-power objective almost touches the slide.

8. Looking through the eyepiece, very slowly turn the coarse adjustment knob until the specimen comes into focus.

9. To switch to the high-power objective lens, look at the microscope from the side. Carefully revolve the nosepiece until the high-power objective lens clicks into place. Make sure the lens does not hit the slide.

10. Looking through the eyepiece, turn the fine adjustment knob until the specimen comes into focus.

Making a Wet-Mount Slide

Use the following procedures to make a wet-mount slide of a specimen.

1. Obtain a clean microscope slide and a coverslip. **CAUTION:** Glass slides and coverslips are fragile.

2. Place the specimen on the center of the slide. The specimen must be thin enough for light to pass through it.

3. Using a plastic dropper, place a drop of water on the specimen.

4. Gently place one edge of the coverslip against the slide so that it touches the edge of the water drop at a 45° angle. Slowly lower the coverslip over the specimen. If you see air bubbles trapped beneath the coverslip, tap the coverslip gently with the eraser end of a pencil.

5. Remove any excess water at the edge of the coverslip with a paper towel.

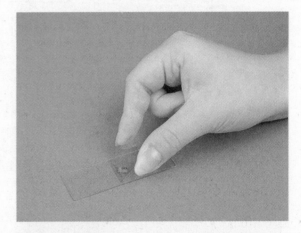

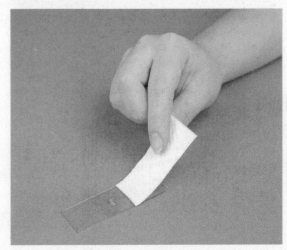

Periodic Table of Elements

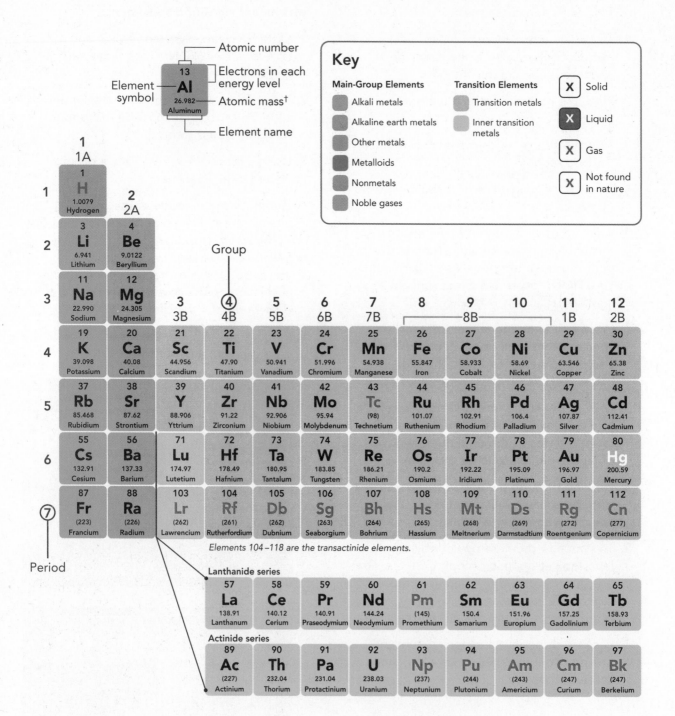

Elements 104–118 are the transactinide elements.

†*The atomic masses in parentheses are the mass numbers of the longest-lived isotope of elements for which a standard atomic mass cannot be defined.*

18
8A

2
He
4.0026
Helium

13	14	15	16	17
3A	4A	5A	6A	7A

5	6	7	8	9	10
B	**C**	**N**	**O**	**F**	**Ne**
10.81	12.011	14.007	15.999	18.998	20.179
Boron	Carbon	Nitrogen	Oxygen	Fluorine	Neon

13	14	15	16	17	18
Al	**Si**	**P**	**S**	**Cl**	**Ar**
26.982	28.086	30.974	32.06	35.453	39.948
Aluminum	Silicon	Phosphorus	Sulfur	Chlorine	Argon

31	32	33	34	35	36
Ga	**Ge**	**As**	**Se**	**Br**	**Kr**
69.72	72.59	74.922	78.96	79.904	83.80
Gallium	Germanium	Arsenic	Selenium	Bromine	Krypton

49	50	51	52	53	54
In	**Sn**	**Sb**	**Te**	**I**	**Xe**
114.82	118.69	121.75	127.60	126.90	131.30
Indium	Tin	Antimony	Tellurium	Iodine	Xenon

81	82	83	84	85	86
Tl	**Pb**	**Bi**	**Po**	**At**	**Rn**
204.37	207.2	208.98	(209)	(210)	(222)
Thallium	Lead	Bismuth	Polonium	Astatine	Radon

113	114	115	116	117	118
Nh	**Fl**	**Mc**	**Lv**	**Ts**	**Og**
(284)	(289)	(288)	(292)	(294)	(294)
Nihonium	Flerovium	Moscovium	Livermorium	Tennessine	Oganesson

66	67	68	69	70
Dy	**Ho**	**Er**	**Tm**	**Yb**
162.50	164.93	167.26	168.93	173.04
Dysprosium	Holmium	Erbium	Thulium	Ytterbium

98	99	100	101	102
Cf	**Es**	**Fm**	**Md**	**No**
(251)	(252)	(257)	(258)	(259)
Californium	Einsteinium	Fermium	Mendelevium	Nobelium

GLOSSARY

A

acceleration The rate at which velocity changes. (17)

C

conductor A material that allows electric charges to flow. (61)

E

electric current The continuous flow of electrical charges through a material. (60)

electric field The region around a charged object where the object's electric force is exerted on other charged objects. (58)

electric force The force between charged objects. (58)

electric motor A device that transforms electrical energy to mechanical energy. (85)

electromagnet A magnet created by wrapping a coil of wire with a current running through it around a core of material that is easily magnetized. (79)

electromagnetic induction The process of genrating an electric current from the motion of a conductor through a magnetic field. (86)

electromagnetism The relationship between electricity and magnetism. (75)

electron A tiny particle that moves around the outside of the nucleus of an atom. (57)

F

force A push or pull exerted on an object. (7)

friction The force that two surfaces exert on each other when they rub against each other. (8)

G

galvanometer A device that uses an electromagnet to detect small amounts of current. (84)

generator A device that transforms mechanical energy into electrical energy. (89)

gravity The attractive force between objects; the force that moves objects downhill. (8)

I

inertia The tendency of an object to resist a change in motion. (26)

M

magnet Any material that attracts iron and materials that contain iron. (67)

magnetic field The region around a magnet where the magnetic force is exerted. (69)

magnetic force A force produced when magnetic poles interact. (68)

magnetic pole The ends of a magnetic object, where the magnetic force is strongest. (68)

magnetism The force of attraction or repulsion of magnetic materials. (67)

motion The state in which one object's distance from another is changing. (5)

N

net force The overall force on an object when all the individual forces acting on it are added together. (9)

newton A unit of measure that equals the force required to accelerate 1 kilogram of mass at 1 meter per second per second. (7)

R

reference point A place or object used for comparison to determine whether an object is in motion. (5)

S

slope The steepness of a graph line; the ratio of the vertical change (the rise) to the horizontal change (the run). (15)

solenoid A coil of wire with a current. (78)

speed The distance an object travels per unit of time. (13)

static electricity A buildup of charges on an object. (62)

T

transformer A device that increases or decreases voltage, which often consists of two separate coils of insulated wires wrapped around an iron core. (90)

V

velocity Speed in a given direction. (16)

W

weight A measure of the force of gravity acting on an object. (39)

INDEX
Page numbers for key terms are printed in boldface type.

INDEX
Page numbers for key terms are printed in boldface type.

CREDITS

Photographs
Photo locators denoted as follows: Top (T), Center (C), Bottom (B), Left (L), Right (R), Background (Bkgd)

Covers
Front Cover: Khm Kvch Kan T Silp/EyeEm/Getty Images
Back Cover: LHF Graphics/Shutterstock

Front Matter
iv: Clari Massimiliano/Shutterstock; vi: Matteo Arteni/Shutterstock; vii: Perry Van Munster/Alamy Stock Photo; viii: Brian J. Skerry/National Geographic/Getty Images; ix: Gary Meszaros/Science Source/Getty Images.

Topic 1
x: Matteo Arteni/Shutterstock; 002: Heiner Heine/imageBROKER/Alamy Stock Photo; 004: Seth K. Hughes/Image Source/Alamy Stock Photo; 006: Marcio Jose Bastos Silva/Shutterstock; 007 CR: WilleeCole Photography/Shutterstock; 007 TCR: Sonya Etchison/Fololia; 007 TR: Dmussman/IStock/Getty Images; 008 BL: Gbh007/Getty Images; 008 BR: Monkey Business Images/Shutterstock; 012: Ian Lishman/Juice Images/Getty Images; 014: Scott A. Miller/ZUMA Press/Newscom; 015: Jim Zuckerman/Alamy Stock Photo; 016: Emma Yacomen/Alamy Stock Photo; 018 TC: WING/UPPA/Photoshot/Newscom; 018 TL: John Ewing/Portland Press Herald/Getty Images; 018 TR: Jim Cummins/The Image Bank/Getty Images; 022 Bkgrd: Hkeita/Shutterstock; 022 CL: BLACKDAY/Shutterstock; 024: Isantilli/123RF; 026 CL: Janet Horton/Alamy Stock Photo; 026 TL: Hero Images/Alamy Stock Photo; 027: Sorin Papuc/Alamy Stock Photo; 028: Omgimages/123RF; 029 BL: Janet Horton/Alamy Stock Photo; 029 C: Jiang Dao Hua/Shutterstock; 030: ImageBROKER/Alamy Stock Photo; 031 B: D. Trozzo/Alamy Stock Photo; 031 TR: Full Image/Fotolia; 033 CR: ScofieldZa/Shutterstock; 033 TCR: Barry Blackburn/Shutterstock; 034: Kuznetsov_Konsta/Fotolia; 038: Robert Daly/OJO Images/Getty Images; 043 BC: Andrey Volodin/Alamy Stock Photo; 043 CR: Koya979/Fotolia; 048: Jason O. Watson (Sports)/Alamy Stock Photo; 049: Gary Hamilton/Icon SMI/Icon Sport Media/Getty Images;

Topic 2
052: Perry Van Munster/Alamy Stock Photo; 054: Tingimage/Alamy Stock Photo; 056: Ali Kabas/Alamy Stock Photo; 061 BCR: Boonchuay1970/Shutterstock; 061 BR: All Canada Photos/Alamy Stock Photo; 061 TCR: Bokeh Blur Background/Shutterstock; 061 TR: Rassul Azadi/Shutterstock; 063: Andy Crawford/Dorling Kindersley/Science Source; 065: Radius Images/Alamy Stock Photo; 067: Siiixth/Shutterstock; 069: Claire Cordier/Dorling Kindersley/Science Source; 071: Bart Sadowski/Shutterstock; 072: Steve Bloom Images/Alamy Stock Photo; 074: Karl Friedrich Hohl/Getty Images; 079 BR: Valentinrussanov/Getty Images; 079 CR: China Images/Alamy Stock Photo; 079 TR: Simon Turner/Alamy Stock Photo; 081 B: Dave Higginson/Getty Images; 081 TR: Hero Images Inc./Alamy Stock Photo; 083: Tom Wang/Shutterstock; 088: Martin Shields/Alamy Stock Photo;

End Matter
102 TCL: Cyndi Monaghan/Getty Images; BL: EHStockphoto/Shutterstock; TL: Javier Larrea/AGE Fotostock; BCL: Philippe Plailly & Elisabeth Daynes/Science Source; 103: WaterFrame/Alamy Stock Photo; 104: Africa Studio/Shutterstock; 105: Jeff Rotman/Alamy Stock Photo; 106: Grant Faint/Getty Images; 107: Ross Armstrong/Alamy Stock Photo; 108: Geoz/Alamy Stock Photo; 111: Martin Shields/Alamy Stock Photo; 112: Nicola Tree/Getty Images; 113: Regan Geeseman/NASA; 115: Pearson Education Ltd.; 116: Pearson Education Ltd.; 117 BR: Pearson Education Ltd.; 117 TR: Pearson Education Ltd.

Program graphics: ArtMari/Shutterstock; BeatWalk/Shutterstock; Irmun/Shutterstock; LHF Graphics/Shutterstock; Multigon/Shutterstock; Nikolaeva/Shutterstock; silm/Shutterstock; Undrey/Shutterstock

Take Notes

Use this space for recording notes and sketching out ideas.

Take Notes

Use this space for recording notes and sketching out ideas.

Take Notes

Use this space for recording notes and sketching out ideas.

Take Notes

Use this space for recording notes and sketching out ideas.